Mediated Learning In and Out of the Classroom

Cognitive Research Program
Division of Specialized Education
University of the Witwatersrand
South Africa

SkyLight
TRAINING AND PUBLISHING, INC.
Arlington Heights, Illinois

Manual Series
Cognitive Research Program
Division of Specialized Education
University of the Witwatersrand
Director: Professor Mervyn Skuy

Cognitive Research Program Manual Team:
Editor: Mervyn Skuy
Coordinator: Mandia Mentis

Marilyn Dunn
Fleur Durbach
Marténe Mentis
Angela Arnott

Acknowledgments:
Financial assistance in producing this series is gratefully acknowledged from:
Center for Science Development, Human Sciences Research Council
SmithKline Beecham
Beckman Instruments (Pty) Ltd.
University of the Witwatersrand Research Committee

Mediated Learning In and Out of the Classroom
First Printing

Published by IRI/SkyLight Training and Publishing, Inc.
2626 S. Clearbrook Dr., Arlington Heights, IL 60005
800-348-4474 or 847-290-6600
FAX 847-290-6609
info@iriskylight.com
http://www.iriskylight.com

Creative Director: Robin Fogarty
Editor: Sabine Vorkoeper
Proofreader: Katherine Schneider
Interior Page Design: Bruce Leckie
Cover and Illustration: David Stockman
Typesetting: Amelia Gordon
Production Supervisor: Bob Crump

LCCCN 96-77677
ISBN 1-57517-059-0

1817-9-96V
Item number 1446

Dedication

This manual is dedicated to Reuven Feuerstein, whose belief system, theory, and parameters of Mediated Learning Experience constitute the inspiration and mainspring for the work of our cognitive research program. We are thankful for his support of our work and the interpretation and applications of his ideas and concepts in this manual.

Contents

Foreword

The theory of Mediated Learning Experience (MLE) dates back to the 1950s. I developed it to explain individuals' different propensities for learning. For example, young adults emigrating from different cultures to Israel have shown different levels of learning propensity in adapting to Israel's technology-oriented society. Some of these differences are explained by the nature of the cultures from which these individuals came. What is more interesting, however, are the differences in the learning propensities among individuals belonging to the *same* culture. In this respect, the observed intragroup differences were often greater than the intergroup ones.

Low-functioning individuals among the culturally different groups were able to adapt to the new culture's stimuli and requirements by direct exposure. Other individuals, whom we later defined as "culturally deprived," were able to benefit not at all or only very little from their exposure to the new culture. They were only able to integrate marginally.

Similar observations have been made by researchers attempting to define the cognitive structure of culturally different groups. The researchers found that there were differences that could not be explained by the culture the immigrants came from. Thus, they dispelled the all-too-often emitted hypothesis that certain cultures "deprive" their members. As a result, we linked the differences in learning propensity to an individual's exposure through MLE to his own culture, irrespective of its nature or level of conceptualization, technology, or institutionalized education.

Culturally different individuals have become "different" by learning their own culture. This learning experience, usually gained through an MLE process, turns individuals into efficient learners. They use their previously acquired learning experiences to confront a new culture. Culturally deprived individuals, on the other hand, have not been exposed to their own culture. They have not learned to learn. Therefore, it is difficult for them to adapt to the new, more complex conditions of life, which require them to use a learning process for which they have not developed the necessary cognitive tools.

Cultural deprivation, in contradistinction to cultural difference, is a universal phenomenon. It can be observed in a large variety of ethnic, socioeconomical, and professional environments. Cultural deprivation and lack of MLE may be determined by (1) exogenous factors, such as cultural environmental conditions, where parents and/or peer groups do not offer mediation or cultural transmission; or (2) mediation that does not penetrate the mental system due to internal physiological conditions. Cultural deprivation (i.e., lack of MLE), irrespective of its etiology, exogenous or endogenous, lowers individuals' flexibility and plasticity. It makes it difficult for them to adapt to new conditions of life through a learning process. Culturally deprived individuals need a special form and level of intensity of MLE in order to overcome these difficulties.

Twenty or more years after its inception, the theory and practice of MLE have become the focus of intensive research. Its meaning extends over large areas of interest in the human condition. Several hundred papers have looked into the relationships MLE has had with other theoretical positions in philosophy, neuropsychology, and cognitive science. These papers addressed not only the possibility of using MLE as a theory to explain the ontology of human cognitive development, but also the possibility of turning the operationalized concepts implied by MLE into guidelines for an applied system. This system would allow individuals to be more adaptable and modifiable, thereby allowing them to confront today's cultural requirements.

Work has also been done by Camusso, Cardinet, Haywood, Lidz, Klein, S. Feuerstein, Rafi Feuerstein, Burges, and Paravy which focuses on MLE's parameters and their relationships to various areas of human development.

In addition, I have contributed to the pioneering work of Yael Mintsker, Nilli Ben Shachar, and others in translating the theory of MLE into operational modalities of interaction between parents and children, caregivers and children, and teachers and students. The Learning Potential Assessment Device (LPAD) manuals include part of this work, as MLE plays a pivotal role in the LPAD. The LPAD includes samples of change in the cognitive structure of an individual. They are interpreted and used as a basis for a profile of the individual's modifiability.

The teacher's guides for the Instrumental Enrichment (IE) program also use MLE as the main modality to shape the interaction of "teacher-materials-exercises-students." The parameters of MLE are used in a focused way in the execution of the IE program.

Mediated Learning In and Out of the Classroom is a continuation of the effort to operationalize the theory of MLE and its various parameters. The great value of this book is that it is presented to the reader as a wonderful paradigm of MLE. A valuable addenda to previous works, it serves educators, parents, and counselors who are applying the LPAD or IE. It is also useful for those in community counseling situations. In general, it is an asset for those trying to find new ways of reaching out to the many people who need a real change in their interaction with their children, students, or peers.

I am gratified by the publication of this book, written by a group of people who have shown their deep understanding and true devotion to the quality of life that can be produced through MLE.

Professor Reuven Feuerstein
Founder and Head of International Center for the Enhancement of Learning Potential
and the Hadassah-Wizo-Canada Research Institute

Preface

The notion that education should develop the cognitive abilities of students, that is, that students should be taught how to think, has been treated in a variety of ways by those involved in education. At one extreme, it has been a notion more honored in its breach than in its observance. In fact, many satirists have portrayed traditional schooling as an antidote to thinking, and thinking as a danger to institutionalized education.

In many countries, the dominant educational ideologies have recognized that to teach children to think would be incompatible with the maintenance of the status quo. In those situations, education does not create thinking students and autonomous learners.

Only relatively recently (in the past decade or so) have practical tools become available that translate the rather pious resolution of "we must teach children how to think" into a practicable activity. Indeed, numerous thinking skills programs have resulted from the increasing emphasis cognitive psychology has placed on the educability of intelligence. Feuerstein's theories of Mediated Learning Experience (MLE) and Structural Cognitive Modifiability have been essential in these developments.

This book attempts to extend the practical application of various dimensions of Feuerstein's theory, especially in relation to Mediated Learning Experience, Deficient Cognitive Functions, and the Cognitive Map. Its production constitutes an aspect of the work of the Cognitive Research Program, which was established within the Division of Specialized Education at the University of Witwatersrand in 1990. Other aspects of the program have included the implementation and adaption of Feuerstein's Instrumental Enrichment Program of Thinking Skills in teachers' training colleges and schools. Their goal has been to develop a viable approach to the enhancement of teacher and child education in multicultural societies. Feuerstein's theory and techniques have served as the cornerstone of and springboard for the work done within this program. I am thus greatly indebted to him and to his team for their vision, their inspiration, and their training.

Tribute should also be paid to the resourceful Cognitive Research team, which brainstormed and researched the material found in this book. The group process by which it was completed, as well as the format in which it is presented—with provision of ample opportunities for independent thought and self-evaluation on the part of the reader—is highly compatible with the philosophy underlying the content of the book itself.

IRI/SkyLight Training and Publishing

Introduction

A teacher recently commented on the report card of an eleven-year-old student in her class, stating that, when he "realized the importance of scholastic achievement," his marks would improve. The response to this teacher is contained in the educational theory and research on which this book is based: only when the teacher realizes that rather than perpetuating the misguided emphasis on scholastic achievement (i.e., tests and grades), the school's task is to develop the student's underlying cognitive functions (i.e., the ability to learn and become an autonomous thinker) and intrinsic motivation (i.e., love of learning and extension of interests), will education improve. Furthermore, the quality of teacher-student interaction and communication will vitally affect the student's development of the cognitive and motivational functions needed for learning. Conversely, it is through the lack of or insufficient mediated learning that cognitive deficiencies arise. These constructs of mediation and cognitive functions are central to the theory and approaches of Reuven Feuerstein.

Who Is Reuven Feuerstein?

Reuven Feuerstein is an internationally renowned Israeli professor of psychology and a scholar in the field of child development. Through his work with low-functioning and disadvantaged individuals, he developed innovative methods of testing and teaching that have been applied worldwide. Along with other contemporary psychologists, he rejects the static belief that individuals are born with a certain intelligence that remains fixed throughout life. In contrast, he has shown that individuals have the potential to change and are modifiable if provided with the opportunities to engage in the right kind of interaction.

Feuerstein has called this "right kind of interaction" mediated learning. Mediated learning permits the individual to develop efficient thinking skills that will enable him or her to become an autonomous and independent learner. In addition, Feuerstein has constructed a list of cognitive functions that are the prerequisites or building blocks of efficient thinking. Together, mediated learning and cognition can pave the way to effective learning.

What Is This Book All About?

This book covers the principles and application of Feuerstein's theories of Structural Cognitive Modifiability and Mediated Learning Experience (MLE). Section I, "Mediated Learning," explains the concepts of MLE; invites participatory learning through interaction; evaluates the effectiveness of a learning experience; and provides ideas for implementing MLE in parenting, counseling, and education.

Section II, "Cognitive Functions and Dysfunctions," explains the cognitive functions and dysfunctions; shows the relationship among the input, elaboration, and output phases of thinking; demonstrates how a teacher might identify a student who is experiencing cognitive difficulties in the classroom; provides strategies for the teacher to overcome cognitive difficulties; and links the strategies of "remediation" to Feuerstein's criteria of mediation.

The ideas and applications presented in this book can be used by anyone concerned with the learning potential of students—parents, caregivers, educators, community workers, school counselors, and psychologists—to:

- encourage autonomous learning
- unlock a student's potential
- promote the use of effective thinking skills
- develop interactional skills
- improve effective parenting
- remediate cognitive dysfunctions
- analyze a student's cognitive strengths and weaknesses
- encourage metacognition—"thinking about thinking"

How to Use This Book

Section I: Mediated Learning

In this section, Feuerstein's criteria of MLE are examined from the perspective of the parent, caregiver, teacher, and counselor. Feuerstein's ten criteria are illustrated in the MLE puzzle on the section cover page. The number of puzzle pieces should not be considered as finite; as new criteria of mediation present themselves, the MLE puzzle should be extended to accommodate them. Furthermore, the individual puzzle pieces do not exist in isolation but should be seen as an integrated whole.

The format is the same for each chapter, each of which deals with a separate criterion.

- each chapter starts with a symbol for and a definition of that criterion
- the Elaboration page repeats the symbol, explains it, provides detailed explanation and discussion of that citerion, and ends with a pertinent quote
- the Example page provides applications of the criterion in the classroom, in the home, and in counseling/community situations
- the Work Pages invite active participation in responding to questions and in applying each criterion to a section of a case study presented in the introduction

- two appendixes close the section—appendix A contains the answers to the work pages, and appendix B contains a rating scale of the MLE criteria for teachers to use in evaluating their teaching according to the mediation principles
- a glossary and references can be found at the end of the book

Section II: Cognitive Functions and Dysfunctions

In this section, the cognitive functions are described within Feuerstein's framework of the three phases of the mental act—input, elaboration, and output. Each chapter deals with one phase and lists and discusses all the relevant functions as follows:

- the Description page includes a quote from Feuerstein that explains an aspect of the cognitive function; a graphic that illustrates an expression of that cognitive dysfunction; a detailed description of the cognitive function; the way in which each function interacts and relates to other functions in the different phases; possible classroom difficulties that a learner may experience; and an example describing a particular classroom difficulty
- the Strategies page provides suggestions for overcoming the deficiencies, linking these to the criteria of mediation that were the focus of Section I (these are not meant to be seen as exhaustive); and snippets of interactions between mediators and learners that highlight aspects of the cognitive functions
- each of the three chapters end with four Work Pages
- three appendixes are included at the end of this section, one of which provides answers to the Work Pages while the other two supply different versions of a rating scale

Mediated Learning

How does learning occur?

Why do some children develop effective thinking skills while others do not?

What can parents and teachers do to help children learn from life experiences?

This section attempts to answer these questions by discussing the theory and providing practical examples of what Feuerstein calls the Mediated Learning Experience (MLE).

Introduction

The mediator enriches the interaction between the child and the environment with ingredients that do not pertain to the immediate situation but belong to a world of meanings and intentions derived from generations of culturally transmitted attitudes, values, goals and means.—Reuven Feuerstein

Feuerstein believes that there are two modalities of learning: a direct approach and a mediated approach.

Direct Approach

The direct approach is based on Piaget's formula of S-O-R, which signifies that the organism (O), or individual learner, interacts directly with the stimuli (S) of the surrounding world and responds (R).

In this kind of interaction with the environment, learning is incidental. Consider the example of a child walking through a garden. The child directly interacts with the flowers and other stimuli. He or she may smell the flowers, feel their texture, or even watch a bee settling on the flowers. While the kind of learning that takes place as a direct result of such experiences is fundamental and necessary, it is incidental and, according to Feuerstein, not enough to ensure that effective learning takes place.

Mediated Approach

Mediated learning is the second, and vital, approach, which ensures effective learning. Here, Feuerstein develops Piaget's formula of S-O-R further to include a human mediator between the world of stimuli, the organism, and the response. His new formula for mediated learning is S-H-O-H-R, in which H is the human mediator. The mediator interposes him- or herself between the learning organism and the world of stimuli to interpret, guide, and give meaning to the stimuli. In this kind of interaction, learning is intentional.

IRI/SkyLight Training and Publishing

Consider again the example of the child in the garden. If the mother were present as a mediator, she would focus the child's attention on specific stimuli and thereby interpret and give meaning to the child's encounter with the flowers. She could focus the child's attention on similar and different colors and textures, thereby teaching the child the important thinking skill of comparing. Or she could interpret the bee's dance of pollination, thereby giving meaning to the bee's actions and showing the interconnections or relationships among stimuli. It is this kind of interaction, in which the mediator intervenes, that results in the child developing a predisposition to the type of learning that is prerequisite for proper cognitive functioning and adaptation to the world.

Both forms of exposure—direct and mediated—are necessary for optimal development. Feuerstein believes that it is mediated learning that allows a child to be more receptive to direct exposure and benefit more from it. This is because mediation is a type of parent-and-child interaction that develops the basic attitudes and competence for self-directed learning.

When a child does not interact effectively with the environment, or experiences difficulties with learning, we develop what Feuerstein calls a "stiff finger." Here, the index finger points stiffly in the direction of the child, indicating that the problem and failure is fixed firmly with him or her. In mediation, however, learning is an interaction between the child and a mediator and fingers point in both directions.

> *The relationship between MLE and the direct exposure modality of learning can be formulated as follows: the more a child has been afforded MLE and the more optimal the mediational process, the greater the capacity of the child to benefit and become modified by direct exposure to stimuli.*
> —Feuerstein 1980, 16.

Ten Criteria of Mediation

To date, Feuerstein has identified ten criteria or types of interaction that are fundamental to mediation. He believes that the first three criteria are necessary and sufficient for an interaction to be considered mediation. The remaining seven criteria may function at different times where and when appropriate, and serve to balance and reinforce each other. Mediation is a dynamic and open process and should not be rigidly applied or seen to be fixed at ten criteria.

The ten criteria of mediation and their corresponding symbols are represented on the following page.

The Aim of Mediated Learning

The aim of this section is to put Feuerstein's theory into practice by applying his criteria to various settings, namely, the classroom, the home, and the counseling/community situation. It should not be regarded as a "recipe book," but rather as a model or a process that describes how interaction can result in effective learning. The criteria are not necessarily new, but are concise, practical, and can be applied in any setting with any subject matter. It has practical application and relevance for everyone involved in education.

TEN CRITERIA OF MEDIATION

Self-Change

Competence

Challenge

Self-Regulation and Control of Behavior

Intentionality and Reciprocity

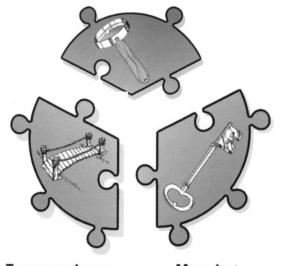

Transcendence   **Meaning**

Goal Planning

Sharing

IRI/SkyLight Training and Publishing

The MLE approach allows anyone involved in a learning interaction to make the "stiff finger" more flexible and thus turn away from focusing on the child and point back and inward.

It should be noted that while the criteria and theory of MLE are based on Feuerstein's work, the elaboration and practical examples reflect our own interpretation and hence may deviate from Feuerstein and other interpretations of his theory.

In an effort to extend the understanding of MLE, the following case study, "A Day in the Life of Alex," will be used to illustrate the ten criteria. Different sections of the cartoon will be discussed on the Case Study Work Pages found at the end of each chapter.

> *No printed word nor spoken plea*
> *Can teach young minds what men should be,*
> *Not all the books on all the shelves*
> *But what the teachers are themselves*
> —Anonymous

A DAY IN THE LIFE OF ALEX

This case study is used to illustrate the criterion of MLE. Different sections of the case study are discussed on the Work Pages of each chapter.

7:30 AM: Alex is depressed! Once again his desire to become a rock star is thwarted by the fact that he has to go to school.

8:15 AM: Music fills Alex's head during math class.

10:30 AM: Alex tells his friends about the song he composed during math class.

11:05 AM: Alex crashes back to reality when he gets an F on his history assignment.

12:10 PM: Alex takes his troubles to the school counselor.

6:00 PM: Back home, Alex reflects on his day.

CHAPTER 1

Mediation of intentionality occurs when the mediator (e.g., parent, teacher, counselor) deliberately guides the interaction in a chosen direction by selecting, framing, and interpreting specific stimuli. Mediation is a purposeful and intentional act in which the mediator actively works to focus attention on the stimuli.

Reciprocity occurs when there is responsivity from the mediatee (learner) and an indication of being receptive to, and involved in, the learning process. The mediatee is open to the mediator's input and demonstrates cooperation.

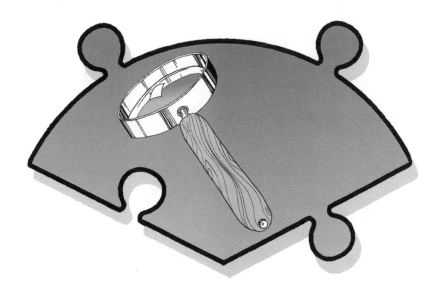

Intentionality and Reciprocity

Intentionality and Reciprocity

It is as if the mediator deliberately holds a magnifying glass up to a particular stimulus in order to bring it into sharper focus and distinguish it from other stimuli. This is intentionality. The intensification of the stimulus catches the mediatee's attention and causes what Feuerstein calls "a state of vigilance" toward the stimuli. This is reciprocity.

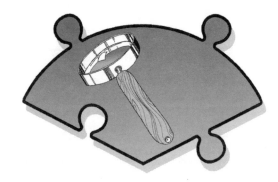

Mediation of intentionality and reciprocity is the first piece of the mediated learning experience puzzle. To learn we need to be able to create significance from the vast amount of stimuli that continually impact our senses. We need to isolate particular stimuli and interact with them. This is achieved through a reciprocal relationship between the mediator and the mediatee. The mediator isolates and interprets the stimuli (intentionality) and presents them in a manner that results in a response (reciprocity) from the mediatee.

Note

- Merely intending to intervene and interpret a stimulus will not guarantee that attention or vigilance will occur (e.g., writing a book does not ensure that it will be read).
- To ensure reciprocity, the mediator should actively seek the mediatee's attention and purposefully impose mediation (e.g., a reader must be drawn to open the book and actively engage in reading it).

In the Classroom

In some classroom situations, obstacles to intentionality and reciprocity may exist. For example, a teacher may wait for the child to initiate an interaction in the belief that it is important *not* to initiate the child's interaction with stimuli. In this case there is no intentionality.

A second situation is one in which the teacher actively invites interaction in a well-prepared, relevant lesson but in which the students don't receive the initiation of the teacher because they are tired, lack interest or motivation, don't perceive the relevance of the given topic, or any other subjective reason. In this case there is no reciprocity.

In the Home

Intentionality and reciprocity seem to begin naturally in the development of a child with the mother's need to interact with her newborn and to engage in eye contact with him or her. The mother gradually directs the child's attention to objects like a rattle or a mobile. In so doing, she frames the stimulus for the child. This, in turn, creates in the child the ability to focus on the mother's face, to establish eye contact, and, with time, to engage in imitation and reciprocal smiling. Thus, the intentionality of the mother evokes the reciprocity of her child and vice versa.

This behavior can be contrasted with that of mediationally deprived children who do not receive consistent nurturing and, as a result, do not develop the ability to engage in reciprocal eye contact. As Feuerstein describes, their eyes slip off your face as if it were glass.

Remember

The three elements involved in and influencing intentionality and reciprocity are

- The mediator—whose language, pace, pitch, and gestures can be varied to enhance intentionality
- The mediatee—whose attention span, interest level, and availability affect reciprocity
- The stimulus (presentation of ideas and material)—which can be varied in terms of amplitude, repetition, modality, etc., to enhance both intentionality and reciprocity

> **"Intentionality and reciprocity are the *main conditions* of an MLE interaction."**
> **—Reuven Feuerstein**

APPLICATION

EXAMPLES

ACTIVITIES THAT WOULD FOSTER MEDIATION OF
INTENTIONALITY AND RECIPROCITY

In the Classroom

A teacher directs attention by framing a stimulus:

"Let's all gather closely around this picture. What colors are in the rainbow?"

☐ The teacher arouses the students' interest and motivation in the subject matter and gets feedback from them.

☐ The students listen to and respond to the teacher in an atmosphere conducive to learning.

☐ The teacher reveals an interest in the students and their work, and shows pleasure when they succeed and make progress.

☐ The teacher is ready to reframe something that is not understood, and takes a special interest in slow learners and passive students.

☐ The teacher is well prepared and the classroom well organized, which communicates intentionality.

In the Home

A mother encourages interaction:

"Let's go play in the sandbox and see what we can make."

☐ The parent encourages the child to take an interest in his or her environment and focuses his or her attention on a specific stimulus (an object, activity, or event).

☐ The caregiver displays an interest in the child and offers empathy and an understanding of events.

☐ The parent varies his or her approach to stimuli in order to meet the child's level of interest.

☐ The caregiver engages in eye contact and encourages the child to respond.

In the Counseling/ Community Situation

A therapist acknowledges involvement:

"Thank you for identifying those problem areas. Let's see what can be done to resolve them."

☐ The therapist invites collaboration from the client in developing therapy strategies.

☐ The counselor creates an atmosphere of concern by using an empathic listening approach.

☐ The therapist engages the client by modeling appropriate behavior.

☐ The community worker encourages introspection into problems and responds positively to ideas for their resolution.

TRUE OR FALSE

Write **T** below the true statements and **F** below the false statements.

1. Intentionality and reciprocity are two sides of the same coin. Essentially, they are the deliberate intention of the mediator to focus the learner/child and elicit a willingness to participate in the learning situation.

   —————

2. Intentionality always occurs when the mediator comes to the classroom well prepared.

   —————

DEFINE

Define intentionality and reciprocity in your own words.

_____

_____

_____

_____

_____

_____

MODIFY

Replace the following statement with one that would improve the mediation of intentionality and reciprocity.

   "Get out your books and start working."

_____

_____

_____

_____

_____

_____

Work Page ....

EVALUATE

Educators of the Montessori method believe that children should be allowed to experiment freely with stimuli and that the teacher should follow the child and wait for him or her to ask for an explanation. Do you think this contradicts intentionality and reciprocity?

_____

_____

_____

_____

_____

_____

_____

_____

_____

_____

_____

_____

_____

_____

_____

_____

_____

_____

_____

_____

_____

_____

_____

_____

_____

CASE STUDY

8:15 AM: Music fills Alex's head during math class.

Answer the following questions relating to this section of the case study. The complete case study can be found on pages 6 and 7.

1. Comment on the teacher's mediation.

   _____

   _____

   _____

2. What evidence can be found in this cartoon section that reciprocity has not occurred?

   _____

   _____

   _____

3. How could the teacher have established intentionality and reciprocity more effectively?

   _____

   _____

   _____

14

Mediation of meaning occurs when the mediator conveys the significance and purpose of an activity. The mediator shows interest and emotional involvement, discusses the importance of the activity with the mediatee, and elicits an understanding of why the activity should be done.

Meaning

Meaning

It is as if the mediator provides a key to understanding the significance of stimuli. The key, or the mediation of meaning, unlocks and interprets the cultural context in which the mediatee is situated.

Mediation of meaning is the second piece of the mediated learning experience puzzle. The first piece of the puzzle, the mediation of intentionality and reciprocity, is concerned with selecting and framing an activity or object. Mediation of meaning is concerned with charging that activity or object with value and energy, which makes it relevant to the mediatee.

The process of investing stimuli with meaning often involves communicating ethical and social values. Mediation of meaning is "the process by which knowledge, values and beliefs are transmitted from one generation to the next" (Feuerstein 1980, 13).

Note

Meaning is mediated by investing significance at both the cognitive (intellectual) and affective (emotional) levels:

- values and beliefs are communicated at the cognitive level
- energy and enthusiasm are communicated at the affective level

In the Home

A caregiver mediates intentionality and reciprocity when preparing a bath for the child by running the water and helping him or her get undressed. The caregiver mediates meaning by encouraging enjoyment of the water and providing reasons for the bath experience. In this way, he or she helps the child get excited about the activity and understand its significance.

In response to critics who ask what right mediators have to impose their values on the mediatee, Feuerstein in turn asks what right they have not to. Consider the following:

- when a mother gives meaning to everything she does, the child begins to want and need meaning in all aspects of life
- the process of investing meaning stimulates the child to ask questions and sets the basis for all further inquiry, future challenge, and possible rejection of that meaning
- without a firm understanding of its environment, a child is not empowered to respond to it—either to accept it or to transform it
- without mediation of meaning the child is deprived of access to cognitively and affectively enriched stimuli

For these reasons Feuerstein believes it is every mediatee's right to receive mediated learning experiences and the mediator's duty to provide them.

Although mediators may choose not to consciously impose their values on the mediatee, it is inevitable for this process to occur to some degree. No situation is value free. However, if the mediation of meaning is not explicit, the mediatee's ability to perceive meaning as being value laden and to critically evaluate situations is reduced.

> "Meaning is the emotional and energetic principle that requires mediators to ensure that the stimulus they are presenting to children gets through. It is the needle that carries the thread through the cloth."—H. Sharron

APPLICATION

ACTIVITIES THAT WOULD FOSTER MEDIATION OF MEANING

In the Classroom

The teacher motivates the lesson:

"We are studying geography in order to understand the physical world we live in."

□ The teacher conveys the importance or value of various subjects to his or her students.

□ The teacher makes explicit the underlying strategies and skills involved in a task.

□ The teacher energizes stimuli by changing their frequency and/or intensity.

□ The teacher uses nonverbal behavior (position, facial expression, level and inflection of voice) to convey meaning.

□ The teacher acknowledges the meaning expressed by the students' responses.

In the Home

The caregiver transmits value:

"We are grateful for rain because we need water to live."

□ The parent explains the reason why certain restrictions are imposed on behavior.

□ The parent conveys the importance of activities through modeling behavior.

□ The parent verbalizes his or her reasons for carrying out daily activities while doing them.

□ The mother encourages the child to seek meaning in order to understand his or her environment.

□ The caregiver shares the underlying significance of cultural events.

In the Counseling/ Community Situation

A therapist justifies an assessment:

"We are testing you to see what things are easy or difficult for you; then we will know how best to help you."

□ The therapist conveys the importance of appropriate behavior in certain situations.

□ The counselor helps the client make explicit his or her value system.

□ The social worker discusses the relevance and value of a particular project and promotes enthusiasm for participating in community functions.

□ The therapist interprets and reflects the feelings of his or her client.

Work Page ....

TRUE OR FALSE

Write **T** below the true statements and **F** below the false statements.

1. Mediation of meaning involves giving reasons for actions.

   _____

2. A child's understanding of his or her world is established through the mediator's explanation of situations.

   _____

DEFINE

Define mediation of meaning in your own words.

_____

_____

_____

_____

_____

_____

MODIFY

Replace the following statement with one that would improve the mediation of meaning.

   "Don't steal!"

_____

_____

_____

_____

_____

_____

                                                    IRI/SkyLight Training and Publishing

EVALUATE

In the 1960s it was believed that parents and teachers did not have the right to impose their values on children by mediating meaning and that foisting a preconceived meaning on a stimulus was indoctrination. What do you think?

_____

_____

_____

_____

_____

_____

_____

_____

_____

_____

_____

_____

_____

_____

_____

_____

_____

_____

_____

_____

_____

_____

_____

_____

_____

_____

CASE STUDY

7:30 AM: Alex is depressed! Once again his desire to become a rock star is thwarted by the fact that he has to go to school.

Answer the following questions relating to this section of the case study. The complete case study can be found on pages 6 and 7.

1. Why do you think Alex's father failed to mediate meaning to Alex in this cartoon section?

   _____

   _____

   _____

2. Cite an example of how Alex's father could have mediated meaning.

   _____

   _____

   _____

3. Could intentionality and reciprocity also be used to solve the communication breakdown between the father and the son?

   _____

   _____

   _____

CHAPTER 3

Mediation of transcendence occurs when an interaction goes beyond the immediate and direct need, thereby enlarging and diversifying the need system of the mediatee. The goal of mediating transcendence is to promote the acquisition of principles, concepts, or strategies that can be generalized to issues beyond the present problem.

Transcendence

Transcendence

Every single activity has in it the potential for transcendence. Transcendence is the bridge that connects related activities and ideas, and links immediate needs to ever-expanding needs.

Mediation of transcendence is the third piece of the mediated learning experience puzzle and transcendence is the third essential criterion for rendering an interaction a mediated learning experience. In essence, any act that is a mediated learning experience must include intentionality and reciprocity, meaning, and transcendence.

Mediation of transcendence occurs when the mediator links a specific issue or activity with others. This moves the learner beyond the direct and immediate need elicited by an interaction and bridges it to related issues and activities. In doing so the mediator enlarges the need system of the mediatee to include the need for understanding, reflective thinking, and forming relationships among things.

Transcendence develops in the child (1) a deeper understanding of the world; (2) a perception of how things are interconnected; (3) a curiosity to inquire and discover relationships among things; and (4) a desire to know more about things and seek explanations.

In the Classroom

In the classroom, the potential for transcendence is limited when the focus is on facts and rote regurgitation of those facts, and when knowledge is fragmented and compartmentalized.

This potential can be realized when the focus is on process teaching—the teaching of underlying skills—and when knowledge is integrated and linked to a broader context.

In the Home

Transcendence in the home is limited when no explanations are given for actions and when no connections are drawn between events. However, when links are made to related events, the mediator transcends the superficial goal.

For example, a mundane trip to the supermarket could move beyond the immediate need of buying groceries by engaging in a discussion about:

- where products come from
- how they are grown and packaged
- the display of products based on various categories
- the value of money
- the role of advertising
- the impact of products on the environment

Remember

Mediation of transcendence involves:

- finding a general rule that applies to related situations
- linking events in the present with future and past events
- engaging in reflective thinking to reach an underlying understanding of a situation
- thinking laterally about experiences and issues

> **"Education is what is left behind when the facts are forgotten."—Anonymous**

APPLICATION

ACTIVITIES THAT WOULD FOSTER MEDIATION OF
TRANSCENDENCE

In the Classroom

A teacher elicits the underlying principle:

*"What rule can you generate
from the spelling of niece,
receipt, and deceive?"*

☐ The teacher connects the subject of the lesson to previous or
future subjects.

☐ The teacher reveals the relationship between specific content
and general goals.

☐ The teacher prefers "why" and "how" questions to "who" and
"what" questions.

☐ The teacher generalizes and asks the students to generalize from
specific instances to the underlying rule.

☐ The teacher evokes the students' need to seek and find complex
relationships by providing bridging examples.

In the Home

A parent encourages generalization:

*"Look at this red flower. What
other things can we find that
are the same color?"*

☐ The parent models a particular behavior and explains to the
child its appropriateness in a variety of situations.

☐ The mother provides the child with the vocabulary to enable
him or her to link related concepts.

☐ The father encourages the child to relate a new experience to
previously acquired concepts or ideas.

☐ The caregiver stimulates the child to explore beyond the
immediate experience, thereby enlarging his or her understanding of the environment.

In the Counseling/ Community Situation

The therapist links skills gained in
therapy to everyday situations:

*"We have discussed the prin-
ciples of effective communication; now try them at home."*

☐ The therapist works on role play within the therapy situation,
then asks the client to try the same behavior at home.

☐ The counselor connects seemingly disparate problems by
examining their common cause.

☐ The community worker facilitates insight into community
systems that can be applied to family dynamics.

☐ The therapist links present difficulties to past experiences in
order to generate alternative solutions.

☐ The counselor interprets a child's problems in terms of family
interactions.

TRUE OR FALSE

Write **T** below the true statements and **F** below the false statements.

1. The parent mediates transcendence when in response to a simple question he or she provides more than the child asked for.

   _____

2. Encouraging the student to find relationships among events is a form of mediating transcendence.

   _____

DEFINE

Define transcendence in your own words.

_____

_____

_____

_____

_____

_____

MODIFY

Replace the following statement with one that would improve the mediation of transcendence.

"We are studying this part of history because it is a high school graduation requirement."

_____

_____

_____

_____

_____

EVALUATE

Teachers are often bound by a syllabus and believe that it is their responsibility to ensure that students pass their exams. As a result, they refrain from engaging in activities that are not part of the syllabus and, thereby, fail to mediate transcendence. They believe that linking the present subject matter to other topics or life experiences might distract the students. What do you think?

_____

_____

_____

_____

_____

_____

_____

_____

_____

_____

_____

_____

_____

_____

_____

_____

_____

_____

_____

_____

_____

_____

_____

Work Page ....

12:10 AM: Alex takes his troubles to the school counselor.

Answer the following questions relating to this section of the case study. The complete case study can be found on pages 6 and 7.

1. How does the counselor mediate transcendence to Alex?

   _____

   _____

   _____

2. Comment on the effectiveness of comparing Alex's predicament to that of a boxer.

   _____

   _____

   _____

3. What other opportunities are there in this cartoon section for the counselor to mediate transcendence?

   _____

   _____

   _____

CHAPTER 4

Mediation of competence occurs when the mediator helps the mediatee develop the self-confidence to engage success-fully in a given act. It is not necessarily the outcome of success that is important, but rather the mediatee's percep-tion of it.

Competence

Competence

The feeling of competence is not necessarily associated with an objective or an absolute definition of success but rather with the mediatee's perception of having been successful. It can be likened to the mediatee's conception of her- or himself as a "star."

Mediation of competence is the fourth piece of the mediated learning experience puzzle. It involves developing the mediatee's self-confidence. Self-confidence is empowering; it facilitates independent thought, encourages motivated action, and contributes to the realization of goals. As such, mediation of competence is an invaluable component of any mediated learning experience.

Competence should be seen in neither absolute terms nor as an innate ability or deficiency, but rather as a process. Competence on a task improves with experience and maturity.

Mediating competence involves instilling in the mediatee (1) a good mental set; (2) a positive belief in his or her ability; (3) the motivation to try; and (4) the determination to persevere.

Ways in which competence can be mediated include

- selecting stimuli within the level of expertise of the mediatee,
- rewarding the mediatee's response to the stimulus,
- making explicit the strategies used by the mediatee that result in a successful experience, and
- focusing on and making explicit successfully completed parts of an activity, even though the whole activity might be unsuccessful.

In the Classroom

Confidence can be eroded easily in the classroom. Educational systems that are competitive and product-oriented often focus more attention on errors than on the steps toward success. When negative attention is directed toward mistakes, students begin to define themselves in terms of their weaknesses rather than in terms of their strengths. This negative perception leads to the type of self-image in which the child believes that he or she is never good enough, irrespective of his or her achievements.

A poor self-image can be responsible for a variety of behavioral problems in the classroom, such as (1) lack of confidence, where students become so concerned with the perceived superior ability of teachers and peers that they are reluctant to attempt or persevere with tasks; (2) lack of motivation, where students avoid or opt out of tasks; and (3) anxiety, resulting in impulsivity and erratic performance.

The perceptions that parents and teachers have of children and convey to them, both explicitly and implicitly, have a profound impact on their sense of competence. Children often live up (or down) to other's expectations, resulting in a self-fulfilling prophecy.

Remember

The various components of mediated learning experience should not be seen in isolation. All ten pieces of the mediated learning experience puzzle complement and balance each other.

For example, the mediation of competence, as a process toward success, reinforces the mediation of self-change, or the perception of inner growth and progress (see chapter 10).

> **"Perhaps the most important single cause of a person's success or failure educationally has to do with the question of what he believes about himself."—Arthur W. Combs**

APPLICATION

ACTIVITIES THAT WOULD FOSTER MEDIATION OF COMPETENCE

In the Classroom

The teacher praises:

"You've done very well on this math problem."

- ☐ The teacher modifies the stimuli according to the students' level of competence by selecting appropriate material, simplifying, slowing down, and repeating.
- ☐ The teacher phrases questions according to the students' level of development.
- ☐ The teacher interprets the reasons for the students' success, and makes sure they understand the processes that lead to successful performance.
- ☐ The teacher makes the students aware of their progress.
- ☐ The teacher responds to positive elements in the students' work, even when the overall results are unsatisfactory.

In the Home

The mother gives reasons for the child's success:

"Well done! This time you held the cup with both hands and you didn't spill any of the milk."

- ☐ The father focuses on the child's good behavior rather than on the bad.
- ☐ The mother does chores with the child's "help" and shows her appreciation.
- ☐ The parent praises the child for applying problem-solving strategies successfully.
- ☐ The caregiver takes the child's level of development into account when structuring an activity.
- ☐ The parent encourages the child to recognize the reasons underlying successful behavior.

In the Counseling/ Community Situation

The community worker praises and reflects on successful intervention:

"Your empathy for children enabled you to settle the dispute effectively."

- ☐ The counselor works through strengths in order to remediate weaknesses, thus ensuring a feeling of competence.
- ☐ The community worker empowers the group members by identifying their particular talents or skills.
- ☐ The therapist helps the child represent progress on a chart.
- ☐ The counselor breaks down a difficult concept in order to make it accessible.

Work Page ....

TRUE OR FALSE

Write **T** below the true statements and **F** below the false statements.

1. The therapist who provides the low-functioning child with a realistic assessment of his or her weaknesses is mediating competence.

   ⎯⎯⎯⎯⎯

2. The teacher should take the students' developmental levels into account when planning activities.

   ⎯⎯⎯⎯⎯

DEFINE

Define competence in your own words.

_____

_____

_____

_____

_____

_____

MODIFY

Replace the following statement with one that would improve the mediation of competence.

"It's not as bad as last time, but try again."

_____

_____

_____

_____

_____

EVALUATE

Our current educational system equates success with getting the right end product. Therefore, rewarding a child for the positive aspects of his or her working process, even when the end product is unsuccessful, is doing the child a disservice because this approach to learning is incompatible with the existing system. What do you think?

_____

_____

_____

_____

_____

_____

_____

_____

_____

_____

_____

_____

_____

_____

_____

_____

_____

_____

_____

_____

_____

_____

_____

CASE STUDY

11:05 AM: Alex crashes back to reality when he gets an F on his history assignment.

Answer the following questions relating to this section of the case study. The complete case study can be found on pages 6 and 7.

1. Comment on whether you think mediation of competence is shown in the above cartoon section.

   _____

   _____

   _____

2. What evidence is there that negative labeling has occurred in the class? What impact does this have on Alex?

   _____

   _____

   _____

3. Do you think it is valuable for students to know each other's grades and class ranks?

   _____

   _____

   _____

CHAPTER 5

Mediation of self-regulation and control of behavior occurs when the mediator intervenes in order to make the mediatee conscious of the need to self-monitor and adjust behavior. The rapidity and intensity of the mental activity is modified according to the characteristics of the stimuli and the circumstances.

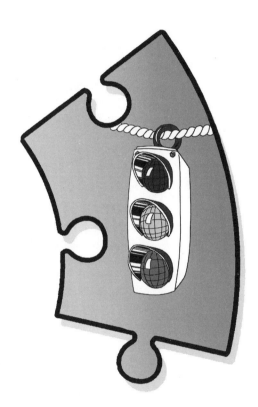

Self-Regulation and Control of Behavior

Self-Regulation and Control of Behavior

Mediating self-regulation and control of behavior can be likened to instilling in a child a self-regulatory traffic light. The red light will stop the child from rushing impulsively into a task or situation, the yellow light will caution the child to engage in reflective thinking about the task, and the green light will encourage the child to go through the activity systematically and appropriately.

Mediation of self-regulation and control of behavior is the fifth piece of the mediated learning experience puzzle. Its aim is to encourage children to take responsibility for their own learning and behavior. It involves teaching children to think about their own thinking (metacognition) and behavior and to choose appropriate responses to a particular stimulus or situation. When we dictate to children how to respond and structure their reactions in a situation, we decrease their chances for autonomy and self-monitoring.

Mediation of self-regulation and control of behavior involves helping the child to analyze a task in order to adjust his or her behavior appropriately. For example, a common or familiar task can be executed more quickly than a novel task, and an easy activity requires less effort than a complicated one. Adjusting behavior in response to the particular circumstances of the task involves (1) restraining impulsivity; (2) breaking down complex problems into smaller parts; and (3) engaging in a systematic approach rather than wild guessing.

In the Classroom

The following examples demonstrate the mediation of metacognition in two different educational settings.

Elementary school students were asked to focus on ways of controlling their impulsivity. Following an explanation of Feuerstein's motto of "wait a minute, let me think" and the traffic light image, they were asked to generate their own self-regulatory approach. The class unanimously accepted the motto "Think before you ink" as their reminder to engage in metacognition.

A group of high school students were told to act as their own teacher by providing written comments that

evaluated an assignment. Initially this proved to be an exceptionally difficult task for the students, who were used to being passively dependent on their teacher for assessments of performance. However, as they became more actively aware of their own learning processes they were able to independently assess the reasons for their success or failure and hence monitor and adjust their own response to a task.

Remember

Mediating self-regulation and control of behavior should be linked to other pieces of the mediated learning experience puzzle. For example, in order to shift the focus of the mediatee from one of being a passive recipient of information to one of being an active, independent, and autonomous learner, the mediation of self-regulation and control of behavior can be combined with mediating:

- competence—where the student's perception of success enables him or her to take responsibility for his or her own learning (see chapter 4)
- goal planning—where envisaging a goal encourages the student to plan and undertake the necessary steps to achieve it (see chapter 8)
- self-change—where the student becomes aware of progress by monitoring behavior (see chapter 10)

> "Man's self-concept is enhanced when he takes responsibility for himself."— William C. Shutz

APPLICATION

ACTIVITIES THAT WOULD FOSTER THE MEDIATION OF SELF-REGULATION AND CONTROL OF BEHAVIOR

In the Classroom

To guard against impulsivity, the class motto is:

"Wait a minute; let me think."

- ☐ The teacher emphasizes self-discipline.
- ☐ The teacher models regulated and controlled behavior by not interrupting student answers, reflecting before answering, admitting his or her own impulsivity, and structuring the lesson.
- ☐ The teacher assists students in regulating behavior by asking them to concentrate on certain subjects, reread paragraphs, think before answering, and check their own work.
- ☐ The teacher encourages students to organize work and plan according to priority.
- ☐ The teacher talks through the solution to problems in order to demonstrate a strategy.
- ☐ The teacher allows students to evaluate their own work as if they were the teacher.

In the Home

The parent helps the child respond appropriately:

"How can we cross this street safely?"

- ☐ The parent demonstrates that rushing into tasks without prior planning reduces the chances of success.
- ☐ The father identifies the steps involved in a complex task that he and the child are completing together.
- ☐ The caregiver models how easy and familiar tasks can be completed quickly while more difficult and complicated tasks require more careful planning.
- ☐ The parent fosters the child's awareness of the consequences of actions and the need to take responsibility for them.

In the Counseling/ Community Situation

The therapist encourages reflective action rather than impulsive reaction:

"Rather than just reacting to your partner's demands, think about a strategy for effective communication."

- ☐ The community worker models careful analysis of a problem as opposed to rushing to quick and easy solutions.
- ☐ The therapist guides the client to recognize the build-up of emotions that lead to antisocial behavior, and the steps needed for its control.
- ☐ The community worker elicits from the group the process by which they solved a problem in order to facilitate taking responsibility for their actions.
- ☐ The therapist helps the client plan a study time table.

Work Page ....

TRUE OR FALSE

Write **T** below the true statements and **F** below the false statements.

1. The therapist who uses professional expertise to provide immediate solutions to the client's problem is mediating regulation of behavior.

   _____

2. The student who checks answers before handing in an exam is demonstrating self-regulation and control of behavior.

   _____

DEFINE

Define self-regulation and control of behavior in your own words.

_____

_____

_____

_____

_____

_____

MODIFY

Replace the following statement with one that would improve the mediation of self-regulation and control of behavior.

"Redo! This work is full of careless errors."

_____

_____

_____

_____

_____

_____

IRI/SkyLight Training and Publishing

EVALUATE

Spontaneity and impulsivity are often seen to be at the heart of creativity. Mediating self-regulation and control of behavior involves restraining impulsivity and engaging in systematic and planned rather than spontaneous behavior. Therefore, mediation of self-regulation and control of behavior could stifle creativity. What do you think?

_____

_____

_____

_____

_____

_____

_____

_____

_____

_____

_____

_____

_____

_____

_____

_____

_____

_____

_____

_____

_____

_____

_____

_____

Work Page •••

CASE STUDY

11:05 AM: Alex crashes back to reality when he gets an F on his history assignment.

Answer the following questions relating to this section of the case study. The complete case study can be found on pages 6 and 7.

1. Has the teacher modeled an attitude that promotes effective self-regulation and control of behavior?

   _____

   _____

   _____

2. Comment on Alex's self-evaluation after he received his grade.

   _____

   _____

   _____

3. Give an example of how the teacher could have responded to mediate self-regulation and control of behavior.

   _____

   _____

   _____

IRI/SkyLight Training and Publishing

Mediation of sharing behavior relates to the interdependence of the mediator and the mediatee, and of individuals in general. It is the mutual need for cooperation at a cognitive and affective level. Sharing develops empathy through social interaction.

Sharing

Sharing

Sharing relates to the intrinsic need for interdependence. It can be likened to two interlocking hearts.

Mediation of sharing behavior is the sixth piece of the mediated learning experience puzzle. It concerns a person's need to connect with others. Feuerstein believes it is "one of the foundations of our social existence" (cited by Sharron 1987, 17).

Mediation of sharing occurs when the mediator and mediatee or a group of learners focus on an activity together and respond together. The mediator shares ideas and feelings and encourages the mediatee to do the same. Sharing is the reciprocal need for cooperation at both an intellectual and emotional level. It involves openly listening to another point of view and being sensitive to the feelings of others.

Mediation of sharing emphasizes cooperation; the result is to promote competence in social interactions by way of the following:

- an environment of trust is developed with mutual self-disclosure
- self-concept is strengthened when successes are shared and failures worked through with an empathic listener
- sharing ideas both verbally and in written form helps develop cognitive processes and clarify confused thinking

In the Classroom

While mediation of sharing behavior is automatically part of any healthy family, it is often ignored or even discouraged in some classrooms. In the traditional classroom, in which the teacher dominates and directs the teaching to the class as a whole, the students become isolated and passive. Student-to-student interactions are minimal and learning is individualistic and competitive.

In order to deemphasize competitive learning in the classroom and, instead, mediate sharing behavior, more cooperative learning could be introduced. This includes group work, peer tutoring, and an emphasis on students as active and social learners rather than passive recipients of teaching.

In the Home

Sharing behavior begins in the womb as a mother shares her body with the fetus. The close emotional bond between child and parent is nurtured through eye contact, and pointing at and playing together with objects. It develops into "give-and-take" interactions, empathic communication, and sophisticated social relationships.

Sharing can be mediated in the home by encouraging turn-taking and cooperation. Sharing the day's events over the dinner table and helping with household chores not only strengthen family relationships but also facilitate the development of social skills.

Remember

All the criteria of mediated learning balance and complement each other. For example, sharing, where interdependence is promoted, is constantly balanced with individuation, where independence of action and thought is encouraged (see chapter 7).

"There is no self without others."—Anonymous

APPLICATION

ACTIVITIES THAT WOULD FOSTER THE MEDIATION OF SHARING BEHAVIOR

In the Classroom

The teacher facilitates interaction:

"Would you and Sue discuss the question and then tell the class your answer?"

- ☐ The teacher encourages students to help and listen to each other.
- ☐ The teacher instills in the students a sensitivity toward others.
- ☐ The teacher arranges opportunities for group activities.
- ☐ The teacher selects subject matter that emphasizes the importance of cooperation.
- ☐ The teacher applies group-teaching methods and encourages the students to share their experience with others.

In the Home

The father encourages the child to relate his or her experiences:

"Tell me about your day at the zoo with granny."

- ☐ The mother facilitates cooperation among family members by encouraging turn-taking and promoting the sharing of chores.
- ☐ The parent models sharing behavior by relating experiences to his or her children and allowing them to share their feelings.
- ☐ The caregiver arranges opportunities for participation in play groups and other group activities.

In the Counseling/ Community Situation

The counselor fosters cooperation:

"Problems are often a lot less complicated if faced together . . . two heads are better than one."

- ☐ The therapist encourages clients to share their problems, seeking commonality with each other and developing support groups.
- ☐ The therapist models empathic listening in a group-therapy setting.
- ☐ The counselor allows the group to experience the benefits of a democratic approach.
- ☐ The community worker initiates discussion about the benefits of sharing rather than competing for scarce resources.

Work Page ....

TRUE OR FALSE

Write **T** below the true statements and **F** below the false statements.

1. The mother who puts away her children's toys is demonstrating sharing behavior.

   _____

2. A lack of mediation of sharing may result in an inability to form friendships.

   _____

DEFINE

Define sharing in your own words.

_____

_____

_____

_____

_____

_____

MODIFY

Replace the following statement with one that would improve the mediation of sharing behavior.

"Finish your project by yourself."

_____

_____

_____

_____

_____

_____

Work Page ....

EVALUATE

Encouraging competition by posting class ranks and awarding prizes prepares students for life in a competitive society. Mediating sharing behavior, where competition is deemphasized, does not help students cope in today's individualistic world. What do you think?

_____

_____

_____

_____

_____

_____

_____

_____

_____

_____

_____

_____

_____

_____

_____

_____

_____

_____

_____

_____

_____

_____

_____

_____

_____

Work Page ....

CASE STUDY

10:30 AM: Alex tells his friends about the song he composed during math class.

Answer the following questions relating to this section of the case study. The complete case study can be found on pages 6 and 7.

1. Do you think sharing occurred in the above cartoon section?

   _____

   _____

   _____

2. Can a peer be an effective mediator?

   _____

   _____

   _____

3. The talent contest suggested by Alex's friend will involve individuation and competition. Are these concepts incompatible with mediating sharing behavior?

   _____

   _____

   _____

IRI/SkyLight Training and Publishing

Individuation occurs when the mediator fosters a sense of uniqueness and difference within the mediatee. Mediation of individuation encourages autonomy and independence from others, and celebrates the diversity of people.

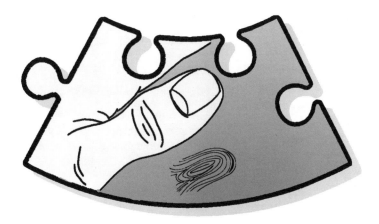

Individuation

Individuation

Individuation can be likened to a thumb-print, which is unique and different for each and every individual. Putting one's own independent and original mark on something would be like leaving one's thumbprint.

Mediation of individuation is the seventh piece of the mediated learning experience puzzle. It involves fostering the development of the individual's autonomy and unique personality. The mediator acknowledges the differences among people due to past experiences, individual abilities, behavioral styles, motives, emotions, and other characteristics, and encourages the mediatee to reach his or her own potential.

Parents, teachers, and caregivers who do not believe in the ability of a child to assume control and take responsibility for him- or herself will stifle the individuation and self-expression of that child. Such stifling of individuation could result in what Hopson and Scally refer to as "pinball living," in which individuals who are incapable of taking responsibility for their lives become like

> balls in a pinball machine (which) have no life of their own; they are set in motion by someone else and then bounce from one place to another without any clear direction, sometimes even making big scores, but then sinking into oblivion until someone sets them off again (Hopson and Scally 1981, 52).

The opposite of pinball living is self-empowered living, which results from the mediation of individuation.

In the Classroom

The educator Belle Wallace describes two opposite teaching approaches. The first type, which Wallace believes stifles individuation, is the inert curriculum. In this type of classroom the teacher dominates:

- teaching is content based and requires the rote recall of facts; and
- students are passive and conforming and have an external locus of control (e.g., need extrinsic motivators)

The opposite approach to teaching, which enhances individuation, Wallace refers to as the enabling curriculum. In this type of classroom

- learning is student oriented;
- teaching is process based and encourages autonomous learners; and
- students take responsibility for their learning and have an internal locus of control (e.g., self-discipline)

Individuation in the classroom requires diversification of the teacher's approach and goals in order to meet students' individual differences in ability and temperament.

In the Home

By mediating individuation, the parent encourages a child to take control and responsibility for his or her daily activities. For example, by trusting the child to take care of his or her own pets, the parent promotes autonomy.

The parent who shows an interest in a child's hobbies will help to develop the unique personality of that child.

Remember

The various pieces of the mediated learning experience puzzle work dynamically to balance and complement each other. The mediation of individuation, which promotes autonomy and independence, is balanced by the mediation of sharing, which fosters cooperation and interdependence (see chapter 6).

> "I yam what I yam and that's all that I yam."
> —Popeye the Sailor Man

APPLICATION

ACTIVITIES THAT WOULD FOSTER THE MEDIATION OF INDIVIDUATION

In the Classroom

The teacher accepts original responses:

"That's an interesting answer. Tell me how you came up with it."

- ☐ The teacher accepts divergent responses and encourages independent and original thinking.
- ☐ The teacher holds the students responsible for their behavior and assigns them responsible tasks.
- ☐ The teacher lets the students choose some of their classroom activities and encourages diversity in their use of free time.
- ☐ The teacher enhances the positive aspects of multiculturalism and ideological and religious differences.
- ☐ The teacher refrains from asking for total obedience and total identification with his or her values and beliefs.

In the Home

The parent praises individual talent:

"Mary, you're fantastic with animals. I'm glad you've decided to become a veterinarian."

- ☐ The parent respects the right of the child to be different—the "free-to-be-me" approach.
- ☐ The parent encourages the child to express some control over his or her behavior, thereby allowing the child to develop his or her own personality.
- ☐ The parent acknowledges and enjoys the unfolding of the child's interests and abilities.
- ☐ The family members respect one another's right to privacy.

In the Counseling/ Community Situation

The community worker models the acceptance of differences:

"Let's examine how our different values influence our perceptions of this problem."

- ☐ The community worker makes explicit the heterogeneous nature of the group and celebrates it as a valuable resource.
- ☐ The therapist encourages parents to develop boundaries among individuals in the family.
- ☐ The counselor helps the client to perceive her- or himself as worthy and competent, yet unique.
- ☐ The therapist bases interpretations on the client's perceptions of his or her world.
- ☐ The community worker encourages self-government by individuals in the group in areas pertaining to their expertise or interests.

Work Page ....

TRUE OR FALSE

Write **T** below the true statements and **F** below the false statements.

1. Acknowledging the differences among individuals is mediating individuation.

   _____

2. Unquestioning obedience to authority is compatible with individuation.

   _____

DEFINE

Define individuation in your own words.

_____

_____

_____

_____

_____

_____

MODIFY

Replace the following statement with one that would improve the mediation of individuation.

"Dad will be so proud when you are old enough to carry on the family business."

_____

_____

_____

_____

_____

_____

IRI/SkyLight Training and Publishing

EVALUATE

Mediating individuation results in selfishness and egocentric behavior and could pave the way for greed and power-seeking behavior. Cooperation and democratic and collective values are incompatible with individuation. What do you think?

_____

_____

_____

_____

_____

_____

_____

_____

_____

_____

_____

_____

_____

_____

_____

_____

_____

_____

_____

_____

_____

_____

_____

_____

_____

Work Page ....

CASE STUDY

6:00 PM: Back home, Alex reflects on his day.

Answer the following questions relating to this section of the case study. The complete case study can be found on pages 6 and 7.

1. Comment on Alex's father's thoughts as they relate to the mediation of individuation.

   _____

   _____

   _____

2. Is Alex's mother mediating individuation?

   _____

   _____

   _____

3. Mediation of individuation involves allowing a child to take responsibility for decisions and become self-empowered. To what extent and in what way is Alex encouraged or discouraged in this regard?

   _____

   _____

   _____

IRI/SkyLight Training and Publishing

Mediation of goal planning occurs when the mediator guides and directs the mediatee through the processes involved in setting, planning, and achieving goals by making the process explicit.

Goal Planning

Goal Planning

Goal planning can be likened to setting your sights on a target and developing a strategy to aim for the bull's eye.

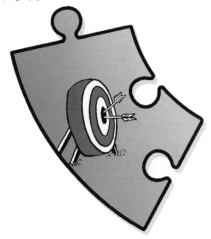

Mediation of goal planning is the eighth piece of the mediated learning experience puzzle. It involves encouraging and guiding the mediatee to set goals, and discussing explicit means for achieving them. Elaboration of the process in goal-directed behavior is equally as important as accomplishing the task. The mediatee takes initiatives in setting, seeking, and reaching objectives.

Effective goals should be:

- *conceivable*—the mediatee should be able to conceptualize, understand, and identify the goal
- *believable*—it is difficult to believe in a goal if you have never seen it achieved by someone else
- *achievable*—be perceived by the student as accomplishable, i.e., within her or his capabilities
- *modifiable*—capable of being monitored and adapted
- *desirable*—the mediatee must sincerely want to fulfill the goal, rather than feel obliged to
- *growth facilitating*—not destructive to the mediatee, to others, or to society

Children can be impulsive; they have a strong desire for immediate gratification. This can manifest itself on both ends of the spectrum—in the overindulged child and in the deprived child.

The overindulged child whose requests are immediately satisfied never learns to delay gratification and engage in long-term goal planning. The deprived child, such as a homeless child, who has to live in the "here-and-now" in order to satisfy his or her basic needs for survival, does not have the opportunity to develop the skills for long-term planning.

When faced with a child in either of these scenarios, the counselor must help him or her to develop the ability to delay gratification and feel more in control of achieving goals through understanding the processes involved. This will lead to greater self-confidence, empathy, autonomy, and more positive, resourceful, and independent learning.

Note

The five aspects of goal planning and achievement are (1) setting goals that are realistic and appropriate to the situation; (2) planning how those goals can be achieved; (3) taking the steps to achieve the goals; (4) evaluating and reviewing the process of achieving the goals; and (5) modifying and adjusting the goals as needed.

Remember

Mediation of goal planning is inextricably linked to the other criteria of the mediated learning experience puzzle, namely:

- *competence*—achieving goals results in a positive self-concept (see chapter 4)
- *self-regulation and control of behavior*—monitoring behavior facilitates reaching goals (see chapter 5)
- *individuation*—setting goals promotes autonomy and uniqueness (see chapter 7)
- *challenge*—the excitement of achieving a goal reinforces a sense of challenge (see chapter 9)
- *self-change*—awareness of reaching a goal develops an understanding of self-change (see chapter 10)

> **"It furthers one to have somewhere to go."**
> **—The I ching 28+32**

APPLICATION

ACTIVITIES THAT WOULD FOSTER THE MEDIATION OF GOAL PLANNING

In the Classroom

The teacher assists in decision making:

"You need to clarify your long-term career goals before you can choose the classes required to graduate from high school."

☐ The teacher models goal-directed behavior by setting clear goals for each lesson and for learning in general.

☐ The teacher fosters the students' need to set realistic goals.

☐ The teacher encourages perseverance, patience, and diligence in the pursuit of goals.

☐ The teacher develops the students' ability to plan, review, and modify goals according to changing needs and circumstances.

☐ The teacher promotes in the students an autonomous attitude toward their future.

☐ The teacher takes into account the students' interests and self-perceptions when helping them set goals.

In the Home

The caregiver elicits a strategy:

"Let's plan how we can raise $50 to donate to the Humane Society."

☐ The parent elicits the help of the child in planning activities.

☐ The caregiver encourages the child to persevere with a task until the desired outcome is achieved.

☐ The father helps the child break down a long-term project into smaller parts and systematic stages.

☐ The parents help the child to reevaluate and set more appropriate and realistic goals when confronted with failure.

In the Counseling/ Community Situation

A community worker encourages reevaluation:

"At this phase of the project, let's review our progress and see if we need to redefine our goal."

☐ The community worker elicits a plan of action from the group—a clarification of the goal, the ways of achieving it, and the possible outcomes.

☐ The community worker helps the individual modify and prioritize goals in order to solve the problem at hand.

☐ The therapist encourages the client to persevere and follow through with the project.

☐ The counselor rewards small advances toward a long-term goal.

Work Page ....

TRUE OR FALSE

Write **T** below the true statements and **F** below the false statements.

1. A poor conception of time interferes with effective goal planning.

   _____

2. A goal is not achieved if the plan is modified.

   _____

DEFINE

Define goal planning in your own words.

_____

_____

_____

_____

_____

_____

MODIFY

Replace the following statement with one that would improve the mediation of goal planning.

"In looking at the results of your career assessment, I think you are best suited for a career in engineering."

_____

_____

_____

_____

_____

_____

IRI/SkyLight Training and Publishing

Work Page

EVALUATE

Consistent planning for the future prevents students from truly experiencing the present. Mediating goal planning results in transmitting neuroses about time, deadlines, and the consequences of actions, all of which stifle spontaneity. What do you think?

_____

_____

_____

_____

_____

_____

_____

_____

_____

_____

_____

_____

_____

_____

_____

_____

_____

_____

_____

_____

_____

_____

_____

_____

CASE STUDY

12:10 PM: Alex takes his troubles to the school counselor.

Answer the following questions relating to this section of the case study. The complete case study can be found on pages 6 and 7.

1. What are the short-term and the long-term goals that the counselor is mediating to Alex?

   _____

   _____

   _____

2. Effective goal planning occurs when goals are realistic and appropriate. How could the counselor mediate this to Alex?

   _____

   _____

   _____

3. Explain the difficulties Alex was experiencing initially and suggest what positive outcome could result from effective goal planning.

   _____

   _____

   _____

CHAPTER 9

Mediation of challenge occurs when the mediator instills in the mediatee a feeling of determination and enthusiasm to cope with novel and complex tasks. Identifying the steps involved in achieving success provides motivation for facing further challenges.

Challenge

Challenge

Mediation of challenge can be likened to exploring new and strange territories. Like climbing a mountain, it requires determination to persevere. The emotional peaks the explorer experiences are the excitement of success.

Mediation of challenge is the ninth piece of the mediated learning experience puzzle. It involves evoking in the mediatee the motivation to attempt something new and the determination to persevere with something difficult. In a world that is constantly and rapidly changing, novelty and complexity become the norm and mediating challenge helps prepare the mediatee to master these changes. It involves overcoming both a fear of the unknown and a resistance toward anything difficult or unusual.

Mediation of challenge can be achieved in a number of ways. For example,

- the mediator can model an open and excited attitude when faced with new and difficult situations;
- the mediator can create opportunities for the mediatee to face novel and complex tasks;
- the mediator can encourage creativity, curiosity, and originality in confronting new tasks;
- the mediator can reward success and reflect the mediatee's feeling of satisfaction and excitement; and/or
- the mediator can encourage sensible and appropriate risk taking in relation to different tasks and situations.

In the Classroom

An overemphasis on grades can have the negative effect of removing the intrinsic value of succeeding at a task. The result is that the student becomes motivated solely by external considerations. In addition, fear of failure inhibits attempts to take on new tasks or to try new and different approaches. The teacher can reduce such fears and mediate challenge by providing practice with unfamiliar tasks and breaking complex activities into smaller and more manageable sections. In addition, he or she could encourage risking initial failure when trying innovative approaches by placing less emphasis on the product and more on the process.

In the Home

We are all born with a natural desire for challenge. Toddlers struggle with manipulating a knife and a fork or with tying their shoes because they want to do these things by themselves. A parent who interferes and does the "difficult" tasks for the child is denying her or him the practice needed to eventually succeed in mastering complex tasks.

Remember

The various criteria of the mediated learning experience puzzle are all related to each other. In this instance, a dynamic tension exists between the mediation of challenge and the mediation of meaning—in mediating meaning, conserving conventional values is emphasized (see chapter 2); in mediating challenge, striving for something novel is emphasized.

> "Novelty is there to be learned and complexity is there to be mastered."—Reuven Feuerstein

APPLICATION

ACTIVITIES THAT WOULD FOSTER THE MEDIATION OF CHALLENGE:

In the Classroom

The teacher reduces anxiety toward a difficult problem:

"These are difficult examples. Let's see how many we can manage."

- ☐ The teacher makes available to students challenging, novel, and complex situations in accordance with their competence.
- ☐ The teacher encourages intellectual curiosity, originality, and creativity, and presents unconventional tasks to students within a nonjudgmental climate.
- ☐ The teacher cites examples of people who have excelled in facing challenging, novel, and complex situations and in overcoming obstacles.
- ☐ The teacher makes the students aware of their growing ability to cope with novel and complex situations by focusing on the positive aspects of their work even when the overall results are unsatisfactory.

In the Home

The parent encourages:

"Try the big slide; you'll see it's a lot of fun."

- ☐ The parent stimulates the child's curiosity and invites him or her to explore new territory.
- ☐ The parents act as models for their children as they challenge themselves in new areas of growth.
- ☐ The caregiver shows excitement and anticipation when faced with a new and different situation, rather than protecting the child from the unknown.
- ☐ The parent provides a choice of activities to stimulate growth beyond the child's present level of development.
- ☐ The parent encourages the child to experience struggling with a difficult activity rather than doing it for him or her.

In the Counseling/ Community Situation

The community worker makes explicit the process for success:

"This new and demanding project will require patience and initiative."

- ☐ The counselor develops the client's confidence to handle complex situations without fear by helping him or her to see them as opportunities for growth.
- ☐ The therapist encourages the client to confront and eventually master situations previously avoided.
- ☐ The community worker models a positive feeling of anticipation in facing a new and changing environment.
- ☐ The therapist provides a nonjudgmental and supportive climate that facilitates experimentation.

TRUE OR FALSE

Write **T** below the true statements and **F** below the false statements.

1. Mediating challenge contradicts the need to conserve the values and attitudes communicated to the mediatee through mediation of meaning.

   _____

2. Breaking a task down into simpler and familiar steps mediates challenge.

   _____

DEFINE

Define mediation of challenge in your own words.

_____

_____

_____

_____

_____

_____

MODIFY

Replace the following statement with one that would improve the mediation of challenge.

"If you don't stick to what's tried-and-true, you will be disappointed."

_____

_____

_____

_____

_____

_____

EVALUATE

Mediating challenge can encourage unnecessary exploration that might go beyond the child's capabilities; this is inadvisable. What do you think?

_____

_____

_____

_____

_____

_____

_____

_____

_____

_____

_____

_____

_____

_____

_____

_____

_____

_____

_____

_____

_____

_____

_____

CASE STUDY

10:30 AM: Alex tells his friends about the song he composed during math class.

Answer the following questions relating to this section of the case study. The complete case study can be found on pages 6 and 7.

1. Do Alex's friends mediate challenge?

   _____

   _____

   _____

2. What does Alex's response tell us about his attitude to challenge? Why does he have this attitude?

   _____

   _____

   _____

3. How could Alex's friend respond in order to counter his feelings of insecurity and thus mediate challenge effectively?

   _____

   _____

   _____

CHAPTER 10

Mediation for self-change occurs when the mediator encourages the mediatee to be aware of the dynamic potential for change and to recognize its importance and value.

Self-Change

Self-Change

Awareness of self-change is like plotting one's achievements and failures on a chart. The overall picture gives an indication of how much one has changed. The responsibility for the fluctuations in the graph, however, lie with the individual.

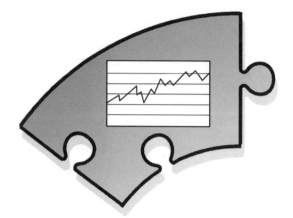

Mediation for self-change develops within the mediatee a responsibility for being aware of continual changes within him- or herself. This must occur if the mediatee is to become an independent and autonomous learner.

Feuerstein believes that human beings are endowed with a propensity for change. It is an inevitable process despite the fact that one may be neither aware of nor take full responsibility for it. In addition, some individuals resist change. For them, it is easier to remain in the "comfort zone," an area where their level of competence is not challenged.

Essentially, an awareness of self-change involves

■ *a recognition of self-change*—that change comes from within oneself;

■ *an expectation of growth*—that levels of competence are always changing and improving;

■ *a monitoring of change*—mapping the changes that take place; and

■ *a welcome of and acceptance of change*—that people are supposed to change.

In the Classroom

The teacher who deemphasizes labels, who believes that ability levels are not static or permanent, and who encourages students to use a progress chart is communicating the value of being aware of self-change.

In the Home

Children love to hear parents and grandparents recite stories of when they were young. The family photo album, a "baby book," and wall growth charts are all items that sensitize children to their growth and change.

Remember

All the criteria of the mediated learning experience puzzle are interlinked. Self-change is linked to

■ challenge—an awareness of self-change makes us less fearful of the unknown and enthusiastic about facing more complex tasks (see chapter 9).

■ competence—an awareness of self-change prevents negatively labeling oneself as a failure. Failure with a task is not necessarily permanent. With experience and practice, failure changes to success. Success is not absolute but relative to previous performance (see chapter 4).

■ goal planning—an awareness of self-change helps one to think about the future and anticipate and plan long- and short-term goals (see chapter 8).

"Change is the most stable characteristic of human beings."—Reuven Feuerstein

APPLICATION

ACTIVITIES THAT WOULD FOSTER THE MEDIATION OF
SELF-CHANGE

In the Classroom

The teacher generates an awareness of
self-change:

*"Your handwriting has really
improved; it's much more
legible now."*

☐ The teacher encourages self-evaluation of individual progress.

☐ The teacher deemphasizes labeling and its consequent self-fulfilling prophecy (e.g., the belief that IQ scores are meaningful).

☐ The teacher helps the students monitor self-change.

☐ The teacher helps the students understand that changing does not make one a different person.

☐ The teacher helps the students to become autonomous learners with internal criteria for evaluating progress.

☐ The teacher discourages comparison of results among students (e.g., class rankings).

In the Home

The parent points out the advantages of
change:

*"Now that you're more respon-
sible you can stay out later."*

☐ The caregiver helps the child monitor his or her development (e.g., by plotting a growth chart).

☐ The parent also experiences change to accommodate changes that occur in the child.

☐ The parent shares positive perceptions of change occuring in the child.

☐ The caregiver makes explicit the benefits of maturation.

☐ The parent encourages the child to compare the progression of his or her report card throughout the school year.

In the Counseling/
Community Situation

The therapist rejects the static perception of the client:

*"It's exciting to see your im-
provement. Let's record it on
your progress chart."*

☐ The counselor instills in the client a desire for self-development by demonstrating how to evaluate growth.

☐ The therapist mediates a sense of optimism in the family's ability to change dysfunctional patterns of interaction.

☐ The community worker assists the group in overcoming resistance to change within the community.

☐ The community worker focuses on the dynamic nature of both the group and its individual members in order to overcome a static and rigid interpretation of problems.

TRUE OR FALSE

Write **T** below the true statements and **F** below the false statements.

1. Labeling a child as weak or exceptional conflicts with the mediation of self-change.

   _____

2. Praising a child for an activity immediately after mastering it mediates self-change.

   _____

DEFINE

Define mediation of self-change in your own words.

_____

_____

_____

_____

_____

_____

MODIFY

Replace the following statement with one that would improve the mediation of self-change.

"You don't have any artistic talent."

_____

_____

_____

_____

_____

_____

EVALUATE

Accepting a child's low level of functioning is the humane approach in teaching. Mediating self-change can raise parents' and students' expectations unrealistically and unfairly. What do you think?

_____

_____

_____

_____

_____

_____

_____

_____

_____

_____

_____

_____

_____

_____

_____

_____

_____

_____

_____

_____

_____

_____

_____

_____

Work Page

CASE STUDY

6:00 PM: Back home, Alex reflects on his day.

Answer the following questions relating to this section of the case study. The complete case study can be found on pages 6 and 7.

1. Self-change involves an awareness that change comes from within. Is there any indication that Alex is open to self-change?

2. Does Alex's mother mediate self-change?

3. How has Alex's self-perception shifted throughout the case study with respect to self-change?

IRI/SkyLight Training and Publishing

Answers to Work Pages

Intentionality and Reciprocity

TRUE OR FALSE

1. True
2. False. It may result in intentionality, but merely coming to class prepared does not ensure that intentionality will occur.

DEFINE

Mediation of intentionality and reciprocity is a mutual interaction. The mediator has the intention to share. The learner wants to receive.

MODIFY

Any statement that encourages more interaction, explanation, and interpretation of what to do (e.g., "Take out your English grammar books and turn to chapter 10. Let's quickly recap what's happened so we can pick up from where we left off.").

CASE STUDY

1. The teacher did not motivate the students and hence did not mediate intentionality effectively.
2. Alex is daydreaming and is not responding to the initiated activity.
3. The teacher could capture attention by asking students whether they understand the exercise or if they need any assistance.

Meaning

TRUE OR FALSE

1. True
2. True. S-H-O-H-R will aid S-O-R. (See Introduction, pg. 3.)

DEFINE

Mediation of meaning means enthusiastically sharing your aims. It answers the learner's questions about why an activity is important.

MODIFY

Any statement that gives a reason or value for not stealing (e.g., "Stealing is socially unacceptable and results in unpleasant consequences.").

CASE STUDY

1. The father's statement fails to explain the relevance of school to Alex's future.
2. The father could have mediated meaning more effectively by explaining how school teaches life skills that are important for any career.
3. Yes. Lack of communication exists because of the breakdown of intentionality and reciprocity. Alex and his father could have discussed the issue further rather than withdrawing into themselves.

Transcendence

TRUE OR FALSE

1. True
2. True

DEFINE

Transcendence is bridging from an immediate experience to underlying principles and related activities.

MODIFY

Any statement that links the study of history to broader "life" goals (e.g., "The past helps us understand the present," or "We can learn to appreciate bias and different perspectives about past events.").

CASE STUDY

1. The counselor bridges Alex's feelings of failure and meaninglessness to a boxer about to give up prematurely. Relating Alex's situation to those of others mediates transcendence.
2. In linking Alex's feelings to the image of a boxer, the counselor may help Alex see things from a different point of view and appreciate that he is not alone in facing obstacles, that giving up prematurely serves no purpose, and that he alone is responsible for changing his situation.
3. The counselor could link Alex's feelings to situations in his past in which he overcame obstacles, or bridge to case histories of how different musicians reached fame.

Competence

TRUE OR FALSE

1. False. Competence means focusing on the positive, not the negative.
2. True

DEFINE

Mediation of competence means instilling in the mediatee a positive belief in his or her ability to succeed.

MODIFY

Any statement that rephrases the comment in a positive way (e.g., "Well done, you've made real progress—but the questions are difficult, so keep practicing.").

CASE STUDY

1. The teacher undermines Alex's sense of competence by neither giving reasons for his failure nor providing guidelines for him to reach or achieve his potential.
2. Alex has internalized the negative label and is living down to low expectations of himself—the self-fulfilling prophecy.
3. Competition is a frequently used classroom assessment technique, but its negative effects include a focus on extrinsic motivation and the undermining of cooperative work.

Self-Regulation and Control of Behavior

TRUE OR FALSE

1. False. The mediator is monitoring the client's behavior and not mediating self-regulation. The mediator is doing it for the client, rendering the client dependent on him or her.
2. True. Self-checking.

DEFINE

Self-regulation and control of behavior involves "thinking about your own thinking" and behavior and modifying your responses.

MODIFY

Any statement that helps the student identify his or her errors and see them as a source of learning (e.g., "See if you can find your mistakes; that'll help you learn where and why you went wrong.").

CASE STUDY

1. No. The teacher passively accepted Alex's poor performance rather than providing strategies for change.
2. Alex internalizes the negative label caused by his poor achievement and does not attempt to find the reasons for his failure.
3. The teacher could work through the assignment with Alex and show him examples of where he might improve.

Sharing

TRUE OR FALSE

1. False. The mother who *helps* her child put away toys is mediating sharing (e.g., "Two hands are better than one"; "If you help me, it'll go quicker"; "I'll help you put away your toys just as you helped me put away the groceries.").
2. True

DEFINE

Sharing promotes sensitivity toward others and emphasizes working together.

MODIFY

Any statement that encourages the mediatee to share ideas, ask for help, or cooperate with others (e.g., "There are lots of sources of information for your project. Ask the librarian or your teacher, or run your ideas by your parents or friends. Talk about your project with others and it'll become clearer, *and* you'll get some new, good ideas.").

CASE STUDY

1. Yes. Sharing occurs among Alex and his friends.
2. Yes.
3. No. All the criteria of MLE complement and balance each other.

Individuation

TRUE OR FALSE

1. True
2. False. Simply agreeing with someone because she or he is in authority does not allow you as an individual to think for yourself.

DEFINE

Individuation is the acknowledgment and appreciation of uniqueness and independence.

MODIFY

Any statement that allows the child to follow a career of his or her own choice, related to his or her own strengths and weaknesses (e.g., "Let's look at your strengths, interests, and values to help you decide on a career choice."). Parents should not be prescriptive or use emotional blackmail.

CASE STUDY

1. Alex's father fails to accept Alex's ambition or recognize his talent and perhaps has his own dreams for Alex's future career that conflict with Alex's. Thus he fails to mediate individuation.
2. Alex's mother's comment illustrates that she accepts and encourages Alex's unique personality and ability; by respecting this right to be different, she mediates individuation.
3. Alex's father appears to block Alex's attempts at autonomy and independence but his mother appears to be more open.

Goal Planning

TRUE OR FALSE

1. True. If you can't think in terms of the future and how the present affects the future then you will have trouble planning long-term goals.
2. False. Goals can be reached irrespective of a change in the plan or the process of getting there. In fact, the plan or strategy to reach a goal often must be altered as obstacles are encountered.

DEFINE

Goal planning is the process by which the mediatee is guided to plan for and achieve goals.

MODIFY

Any statement that would allow the student to formulate his or her long-term goals and establish the steps needed to reach that goal (e.g., "You seem to have strengths in the mechanical area. If you want to follow a career in that direction, what steps will you have to take?").

CASE STUDY

1. Success at school is the short-term goal that will help achieve the long-term career goal of becoming a musician.
2. Alex's strengths, weaknesses, abilities, and difficulties need to be accurately assessed in order to make realistic and appropriate recommendations for achieving his goals.
3. Alex appeared trapped in the "here and now," where he was not focusing on the consequences of his failure and negative attitude. An orientation to future outcomes could lead to greater self-confidence, finding meaning for his school work, and a more positive and resourceful attitude.

Challenge

TRUE OR FALSE

1. False. Challenge complements mediation of meaning. "Culture" is not static and while mediation of meaning transmits dominant cultural norms, a challenge of those traditions is central to MLE.
2. True. Difficult tasks can be simplified by breaking them up into smaller, easier steps.

DEFINE

Challenge is the feeling of excitement when confronting a new and difficult task.

MODIFY

Any statement that encourages students to try new and alternative methods when confronting difficult tasks (e.g., "It will be exciting to try a new approach to this difficult task and see how well we do.").

CASE STUDY

1. Yes. Alex's friend mediates challenge and Alex responds negatively.
2. Alex's response indicates that he does not have enough self-confidence to rise to a challenge.
3. Alex's friends could motivate him by showing enthusiasm and helping him anticipate success.

Self-Change

TRUE OR FALSE

1. True. Labeling a child limits his or her chances for change (e.g., "He is bad at math," results in the self-fulfilling prophecy of the child believing that he is "bad" and performing "poorly.").
2. True. The child couldn't perform the task before and now he or she has new expertise or maturity (i.e., he or she has changed and rewarding this mediates self-change).

DEFINE

Self-change is the recognition, acceptance, and monitoring of continual change that occurs within oneself.

MODIFY

Any statement that encourages the student to try to change or improve (e.g., "That's a good attempt and with practice you will improve.").

CASE STUDY

1. Alex's reflection on the lyrics of the song indicates that he is developing an awareness of self-change and is taking responsibility for monitoring his own growth and change in attitude and behavior.
2. Alex's mother recounts events of Alex's childhood, thus helping him to develop an orientation to time and encouraging an expectation and acceptance of maturation and growth.
3. At the breakfast table Alex was stuck on the frustration of not being able to see the relevance of school and on the unaccommodating attitude of his father. He was unable to perceive any course of action to change the situation. After Alex got a failing grade on his history assignment, he felt stuck with the label of being a failure and that he would always be one. At the end of the case study Alex begins to realize that levels of competence are continually changing and he takes responsibility for his growth and change.

Rating Scale

Mediated Learning Experience Rating Scale

This rating scale comprises a list of mediational activities that may occur in a classroom. The activities are grouped into ten sections according to the main criterion of MLE.

The rating scale offers the opportunity to rate the quality of mediation being exercised by a mediator, such as a teacher.

RATING

The evaluation should be carried out using the following ratings:

- No opportunity = The lesson did not permit the occurrence of the MLE activity/approach

- Missed opportunity = The teacher did not implement the MLE activity/approach when the situation allowed for it

- Usually implemented = The MLE activity was consistently and successfully implemented

- Sometimes implemented = The MLE activity was occasionally implemented

- Negation = The teacher's activity/approach was insufficient or in opposition to MLE

The activities/approaches under each criterion are not exhaustive. Any additional or different examples can be listed under the heading "Other."

DESCRIPTION OF MLE ACTIVITY	NO OPPORTUNITY	MISSED OPPORTUNITY	USUALLY IMPLEMENTED	SOMETIMES IMPLEMENTED	NEGATION	DESCRIPTION OF ACTIVITY WHICH IS INSUFFICIENT OR IN CONTRADICTION TO MLE

Intentionality and Reciprocity

DESCRIPTION OF MLE ACTIVITY						DESCRIPTION OF ACTIVITY WHICH IS INSUFFICIENT OR IN CONTRADICTION TO MLE
1. Teacher arouses students' interest and motivation						1. Teacher fails to engage students
2. Students ask questions relevant to the subject matter						2. Students do not participate in relevant discussion
3. Teacher gives appropriate feedback to students' verbal contribution						3. Teacher is insensitive to students' verbal contribution
4. Teacher gives appropriate feedback to students' written contribution						4. Teacher fails to meaningfully comment on students' written contribution
5. Teacher is willing to reexplain when work is not understood						5. Teacher is not cognizant of the need for reexplanation
6. Teacher comes prepared and creates a sense of anticipation by changing classroom atmosphere						6. Teacher does not prepare adequately for the lesson and fails to create enthusiasm
7. Other:						7. Other:

Meaning

DESCRIPTION OF MLE ACTIVITY						DESCRIPTION OF ACTIVITY WHICH IS INSUFFICIENT OR IN CONTRADICTION TO MLE
1. The teacher explains the importance or value of a subject						1. The teacher fails to provide the purpose or relevance of activities or subjects
2. The teacher explains the reason for focusing on a subject						2. The teacher focuses on a subject without giving explicit reasons
3. The teacher transforms material by changing frequency and/or intensity of presentation						3. The teacher fails to vary presentation, which would convey to students the importance or value of a subject
4. The teacher gives positive or negative feedback to student responses						4. The teacher responds indifferently to student responses
5. The teacher asks "how" and "why" questions—process questions						5. The teacher asks more "who" and "what" questions—content questions
6. Other:						6. Other:

DESCRIPTION OF MLE ACTIVITY	NO OPPORTUNITY	MISSED OPPORTUNITY	USUALLY IMPLEMENTED	SOMETIMES IMPLEMENTED	NEGATION	DESCRIPTION OF ACTIVITY WHICH IS INSUFFICIENT OR IN CONTRADICTION TO MLE

Transcendence

1. The teacher explains a concept or principle beyond the scope of the present subject matter						1. The teacher fails to bridge concepts to related subject matter
2. The teacher relates the subject of a lesson to previous or future subjects						2. The teacher presents each subject as an isolated and unrelated set of information and ideas
3. The teacher explains how the underlying process to solving a problem can be applied to a variety of situations						3. The teacher fails to show how one problem-solving approach can be applied to a variety of situations
4. The teacher promotes the use of work habits that are useful beyond present needs						4. The teacher fails to show how specific work habits may be used in a different context
5. Other:						5. Other:

Competence

1. The teacher selects and presents material appropriate to the students' levels of development						1. The teacher fails to take into account the students' levels of development when selecting and presenting material
2. The teacher phrases questions according to the students' levels of competence						2. The teacher's questions are not presented at an appropriate level
3. The teacher encourages students to be aware of their progress relative to their own standards						3. The teacher measures student progress only according to the class average
4. The teacher breaks down a complex task into its simpler parts in order to reduce anxiety						4. The teacher fails to reduce anxiety by showing how a complex task can be simplified
5. The teacher praises successful steps toward completing a task						5. The teacher praises only the successful completion of a task
6. The teacher rewards participation in an activity						6. The teacher does not reward participation in an activity
7. Other:						7. Other:

IRI/SkyLight Training and Publishing

DESCRIPTION OF MLE ACTIVITY	NO OPPORTUNITY	MISSED OPPORTUNITY	USUALLY IMPLEMENTED	SOMETIMES IMPLEMENTED	NEGATION	DESCRIPTION OF ACTIVITY WHICH IS INSUFFICIENT OR IN CONTRADICTION TO MLE

Self-Regulation and Control of Behavior

1. The teacher instills in the students behavior conducive to learning—good classroom management						1. The teacher fails to instill in the students behavior conducive to learning—bad classroom management
2. The teacher restrains the inappropriate impulsiveness of students						2. The teacher fails to check inappropriate impulsiveness
3. The teacher encourages self-discipline						3. The teacher fails to encourage self-discipline
4. The teacher models respect, commitment, and perseverance in classroom activities						4. The teacher fails to demonstrate sustained interest and commitment in classroom activities
5. Other:						5. Other:

Sharing

1. The teacher applies effective group-teaching methods						1. The teacher fails to apply effective group-teaching methods
2. The teacher encourages students to share their work experiences with each other						2. The teacher discourages students from working cooperatively
3. The teacher shares his or her approach to solving tasks with students						3. The teacher fails to verbalize (talk through) his or her problem-solving strategy
4. The teacher encourages students to help each other and facilitates peer tutoring						4. The teacher always insists on individual work
5. The teacher encourages students to listen to each other						5. The teacher fails to encourage active listening when other students are responding
6. The teacher encourages students to empathize with the feelings of others						6. The teacher fails to promote in the students a tolerance and understanding of another's point of view
7. The teacher selects subject matter that emphasizes the importance of cooperation						7. The teacher encourages competition to the detriment of cooperation
8. Other:						8. Other:

DESCRIPTION OF MLE ACTIVITY	NO OPPORTUNITY	MISSED OPPORTUNITY	USUALLY IMPLEMENTED	SOMETIMES IMPLEMENTED	NEGATION	DESCRIPTION OF ACTIVITY WHICH IS INSUFFICIENT OR IN CONTRADICTION TO MLE

Individuation

1. The teacher accepts divergent approaches to problem solving						1. The teacher communicates that there is only one correct way to solve a problem
2. The teacher encourages independent and original thinking and provides opportunities for innovative work						2. The teacher promotes conformity and discourages individual creativity
3. The teacher lets students choose part of their classroom activities and encourages diversity in the use of free time						3. The teacher is not receptive to students' suggestions and promotes uniformity of activities
4. The teacher enhances positive aspects of multiculturalism						4. The teacher exhibits cultural bias and does not integrate different world views
5. The teacher supports the right of the student to be different						5. The teacher fails to promote acceptance of individual differences
6. The teacher refrains from asking for total identification with his or her values and beliefs						6. The teacher insists on total identification with his or her values and beliefs
7. Other:						7. Other:

Goal Planning

1. The teacher fosters the students' need and ability to set realistic goals						1. The teacher's inappropriate expectations result in the students setting unrealistic goals
2. The teacher encourages perseverance and patience in the pursuit of goals						2. The teacher allows the students to give up on a task as soon as it becomes difficult
3. The teacher explains to students the strategy underlying goal planning						3. The teacher fails to demonstrate the process of setting and achieving goals
4. The teacher develops in the students the need and ability to review and modify goals according to changing needs and circumstances						4. The teacher fails to develop in the students the need and ability to review and modify goals according to changing needs and circumstances
5. The teacher models goal-directed behavior by setting clear goals for each lesson and for learning in general						5. The teacher has no clear objectives and fails to provide a structure for reaching them
6. The teacher instills an autonomous attitude in students about their future						6. The teacher is prescriptive and makes decisions for the students' futures
7. Other:						7. Other:

DESCRIPTION OF MLE ACTIVITY	NO OPPORTUNITY	MISSED OPPORTUNITY	USUALLY IMPLEMENTED	SOMETIMES IMPLEMENTED	NEGATION	DESCRIPTION OF ACTIVITY WHICH IS INSUFFICIENT OR IN CONTRADICTION TO MLE

Challenge

DESCRIPTION OF MLE ACTIVITY						DESCRIPTION OF ACTIVITY WHICH IS INSUFFICIENT OR IN CONTRADICTION TO MLE
1. The teacher encourages intellectual curiosity						1. The teacher does not encourage intellectual curiosity
2. The teacher encourages originality and creativity						2. The teacher instills conformist behavior and discourages divergent thinking
3. The teacher makes available to the students challenging, novel, and complex situations						3. The teacher adheres to the "tried-and-tested" approach and presents conventional tasks to students
4. The teacher encourages students to create their own examples and to present them to the class						4. The teacher inhibits original approaches when engaging in an activity
5. The teacher helps the students anticipate the satisfaction of completing a task						5. The teacher fails to promote intrinsic motivation to complete a complex task
6. The teacher encourages students to persevere with difficult tasks						6. The teacher fails to instill perseverance with difficult tasks
7. Other:						7. Other:

Self-Change

DESCRIPTION OF MLE ACTIVITY						DESCRIPTION OF ACTIVITY WHICH IS INSUFFICIENT OR IN CONTRADICTION TO MLE
1. The teacher promotes self-evaluation of individual progress						1. The teacher fails to develop an awareness of self-evaluation and individual progress
2. The teacher discourages students from using external criteria for measuring progress						2. The teacher explicitly evaluates students relative to class standards and encourages comparison of grades
3. The teacher deemphasizes labeling of students						3. The teacher's consistent use of labeling results in the students acting out these expectations
4. The teacher generates an awareness of change within oneself, and in relationships with others and the environment						4. The teacher fails to create an awareness of change within oneself and in relationships with others and the environment
5. The teacher models self-change by sharing his or her growth and learning experiences						5. The teacher fails to modify his or her attitudes or approaches to new situations
6. Other:						6. Other:

Section II

Cognitive Functions and Dysfunctions

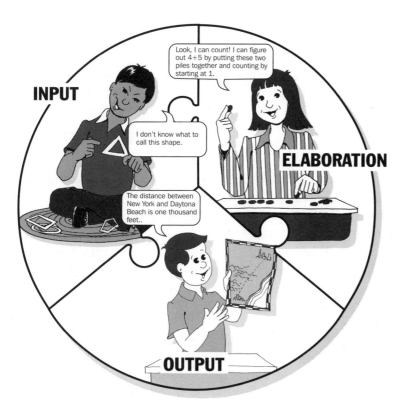

What is cognition?

What are the prerequisites of thinking?

What does it mean to think about thinking, i.e., to engage in metacognition?

How can parents and teachers help children learn how to learn?

This section attempts to answer these questions by discussing Feuerstein's list of cognitive functions and dysfunctions.

Introduction

This section is devoted to an elaboration of the cognitive functions/dysfunctions as identified by Reuven Feuerstein. It is not meant as a substitute for Feuerstein's own program of Instrumental Enrichment, which remains one of the best researched, most promising, and most well-developed vehicles for teacher-student mediation and the development of cognitive functions.

It is recognized that many of the cognitive functions presented in this section may already be addressed by teachers, who may use some of the strategies presented here and/or their own. This section is presented to supplement the teacher's repertoire of strategies, and his or her understanding of cognitive functions. Most importantly, the focus on cognitive functions and strategies for their enhancement is meant to bring it to the attention of teachers, so that they can increase their awareness of, and thinking about, the processes and purposes of education, and the most effective strategies for developing these processes and achieving their goals.

Furthermore, the analysis and undertaking of cognitive functioning in terms of underlying processes is seen as a more effective alternative to the traditional forms of psychometric assessment, which emphasize the quantification of children's abilities, a global approach to their measurement, and provide little link between assessment and intervention. Thus, this section is seen as providing the teacher with a tool to constructively assess and intervene in areas of difficulty.

At the same time, this section is relevant to students across the spectrum of ability, in that cognitive functions can always be enhanced. Moreover, a higher achieving student is not necessarily one who has developed those cognitive functions needed for autonomous learning in later life. Again, cognitive ability is relative, and there will be variations both within individuals (often marked) and across individuals in the degree of competence in any given function. There are also those for whom particular cognitive dysfunctions may be extremely difficult to remediate. In such cases, it is important to adopt a flexible approach, and to find compensatory cognitive functions by which the student can achieve the same goals.

Finally, cognitive functions cannot be seen out of their cultural, developmental, situational, and emotional contexts. For example, what is considered necessary and/ or desirable in one culture may be seen as irrelevant in another; what may be regarded as a deficiency at one age will be considered as developmentally appropriate at another; a student may exercise a cognitive function fully in one situation but, for motivational or emotional reasons, negate it in another. The issue may not relate to the student's cognitive functions at all, but may pertain to the characteristics/ demands of the environment.

Thus, this section's cognitive functions and strategies are not presented in a prescriptive or diagnostic manner. They are meant as a guide to the goals and methods that teachers may adopt in enhancing cognitive functioning.

The list of cognitive functions is helpful in identifying and understanding the reasons for an individual's failure or poor performance on task. Once the deficient functions have been identified, the individual may be helped by correcting and redeveloping these cognitive functions through appropriate and sufficient mediation. Thus, Feuerstein's list of cognitive functions, which is the core of his model of thinking, serves as a very useful assessment and teaching tool.

Aim of Cognition

The aim of this section is to explain and operationalize the cognitive functions and dysfunctions. It provides:
- a detailed discussion of each cognitive function
- practical examples of the cognitive dysfunctions
- strategies for remediating the dysfunction in terms of MLE

We believe that Feuerstein's list of the cognitive functions, which is the prerequisite of cognition, is a valuable tool for:
- diagnosing errors in thinking
- remediating dysfunction
- enriching the cognitive function

This list can be used to help students become more autonomous and independent learners through being aware of and understanding their own thinking and behavior, i.e., exercising metacognition, or . . .

Thinking about their own thinking!

Cognitive Functions and Dysfunctions: Input, Elaboration, and Output

All too often, a child's failure to perform a given operation, whether in the classroom or test situation, is attributed either to a lack of knowledge of the principles involved in the operation or, even worse, to a low intelligence that precludes his understanding of the principles. What is overlooked is that the deficiency may reside not in the operational level or in the specific content of the child's thought processes but in the underlying functions upon which successful performance of cognitive operations depends.
    —Feuerstein 1980, 71

Feuerstein has categorized the cognitive functions according to the three major phases of the mental act—namely input, elaboration, and output. Although artificially separated into three phases, they don't necessarily occur separately in life. However, the subdivision is useful for analysis and description of thinking and determination of difficulties impeding thinking. This model can be used by teachers and parents to better understand and help the child who is experiencing difficulties with a particular task.

For example, if a child fails in the task of classification, it is not enough to comment on the child's poor intelligence or inability to classify—but rather, the underlying causes of the difficulty, which can be found in one of the three phases of thinking, should be sought. The inability to classify, for instance, may be due to underlying functions such as imprecise data gathering at the input phase, an inability to compare the items at the elaboration phase, or poor communication skills at the output phase.

A detailed analysis of a student's cognitive functions requires an indepth understanding of the three phases of the mental act:

Input Phase—Taking in Information (Reception)

This is the phase in which information or data is gathered in order to solve a task. For example, it may involve efficient and accurate perception, adequate listening skills, good understanding of the language and of the concepts of time, space, and quantity, as well as the ability to collect and examine many sources of information at one time.

Elaboration Phase—Working on the Problem (Processing)

This is the phase where the information or data is processed. Our minds work on the information we have gathered. For example, it may involve defining the task, comparing and integrating relevant sources of information, planning, hypothesizing, and working through problems logically, etc. This is the most important and central phase.

Output Phase—Communicating a Response (Expression)

This is the phase where the information or data is communicated or presented. Responses or answers to a problem are given. It involves accurate, appropriate, and efficient communication skills.

Affective-Motivational Factors

Feuerstein's model of thinking implicitly includes affective-motivational factors. This emotional component is central to thinking and learning. It is the motivation and energy for cognitive functions and manifests as the intrinsic need to perform a certain task.

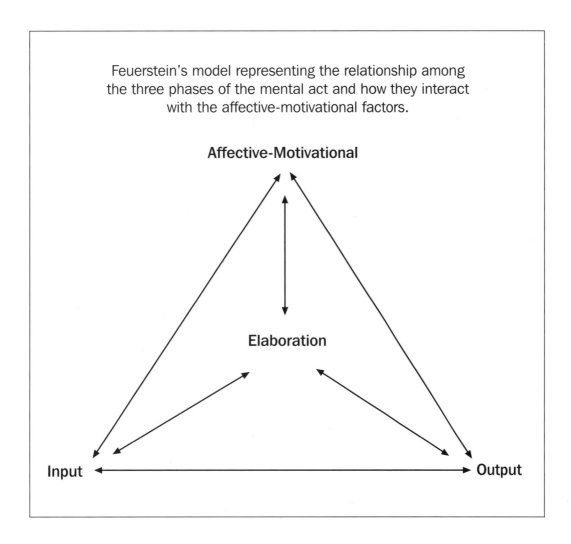

Feuerstein's model representing the relationship among the three phases of the mental act and how they interact with the affective-motivational factors.

INPUT	
Functions	**Dysfunctions**
Perception	
Clear	Blurred and Sweeping
Exploration of a Learning Situation	
Systematic	Impulsive
Receptive Verbal Tools and Concepts	
Precise and Accurate	Impaired
Understanding of Spatial Concepts	
Well Developed	Impaired
Understanding of Temporal Concepts	
Well Developed	Lack of or Impaired
Ability to Conserve Constancies	
Well Developed	Impaired
Data Gathering	
Precise and Accurate	Impaired
Capacity to Consider More than One Source of Information	
Well Developed	Impaired

IRI/SkyLight Training and Publishing

ELABORATION

Functions	Dysfunctions
Definition of the Problem	
Accurate	Inaccurate
Select Relevant Cues	
Ability	Inability
Engage in Spontaneous Comparative Behavior	
Ability to	Inability to
Mental Field	
Broad and Wide	Narrow and Limited
Spontaneous Summative Behavior	
Need for	Impaired Need for
Project Virtual Relationships	
Ability to	Inability to
Logical Evidence	
Need for	Lack of Need for
Internalize Events	
Abilty to	Inability to
Inferential-Hypothetical Thinking	
Ability to Use	Restricted Use of
Strategies for Hypothesis Testing	
Ability to Use	Impaired Ability to Use
Planning Behavior	
Need for	Lack of
Elaboration of Cognitive Categories	
Adequate	Impaired
Grasp of Reality	
Meaningful	Episodic

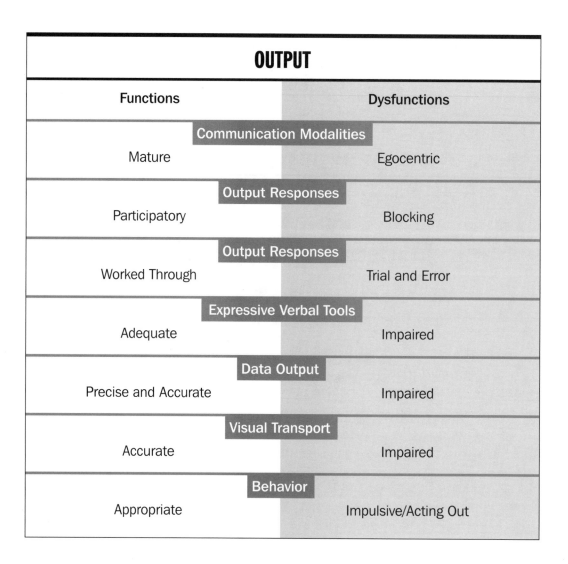

OUTPUT

Functions	Dysfunctions
Communication Modalities	
Mature	Egocentric
Output Responses	
Participatory	Blocking
Output Responses	
Worked Through	Trial and Error
Expressive Verbal Tools	
Adequate	Impaired
Data Output	
Precise and Accurate	Impaired
Visual Transport	
Accurate	Impaired
Behavior	
Appropriate	Impulsive/Acting Out

IRI/SkyLight Training and Publishing

If one were to overhear some or all of these comments about a student's thinking, it is likely that the student is experiencing difficulty at the input phase of the thinking process.

"You've left out five important details."

"Don't just guess; examine it in detail."

"Look carefully now."

"Are you lost?"

"Slow down; take your time."

"You must learn to look before you leap."

"Did you understand the story we read?"

"What were the instructions?"

"You need to work out a study timetable."

"It's the same picture, only seen from a different angle."

"Late again!"

"Which is your right hand?"

"Let's figure out what stayed the same and what changed."

"You'll need to consider different points of view."

"Your essay is off the mark."

"These are just careless and silly mistakes."

Input

Input Phase

The "input," "elaboration," and "output" topography of an intellectual act has an obvious analogy with computer systems, and Feuerstein admits that, despite its comparative sophistication, it is still an over-mechanical analysis of the way children think. However, it has allowed Feuerstein to progress from general analysis and description of the causes of inadequate intellectual functioning in children to a system of diagnosis which can be picked up and used by teachers, parents, and other professionals with a limited amount of training.

—H. Sharron

Feuerstein has grouped the processes underlying thinking, the cognitive functions, into three phases—input, elaboration, and output.

- At the input phase, information is gathered in order to undertake a task or solve a problem.
- At the elaboration phase, information is processed.
- At the output phase, the response is communicated.

At the input phase, stimuli around us are absorbed by our sense of sight, smell, taste, touch, and hearing. Difficulties experienced at this stage will affect how the task is tackled at the elaboration phase and how the product is expressed or presented at the output phase. For example, a student with difficulties at the input phase may rush blindly into a task without taking the time to examine all the necessary information. He or she may often be late, get lost, misunderstand verbal instructions, or have difficulty following a story. Such a student may make careless mistakes, leave out important details, or fail to see the similarities among stimuli.

This chapter deals with problems at the input phase of thinking. A detailed explanation of how to identify each dysfunction is provided and suggestions are made for correcting it using Feuerstein's criteria of mediation.

INPUT	
Functions	**Dysfunctions**
Perception	
Clear	Blurred and Sweeping
Exploration of a Learning Situation	
Systematic	Impulsive
Receptive Verbal Tools and Concepts	
Precise and Accurate	Impaired
Understanding of Spatial Concepts	
Well Developed	Impaired
Understanding of Temporal Concepts	
Well Developed	Lack of or Impaired
Ability to Conserve Constancies	
Well Developed	Impaired
Data Gathering	
Precise and Accurate	Impaired
Capacity to Consider More than One Source of Information	
Well Developed	Impaired

Perception

What characterizes blurred perception is a poverty of details or their lack of clarity . . . and an incompleteness of the data necessary for proper distinction and description.
        —*Feuerstein 1980, 76*

The student's sweeping perception causes her to misread:

> I thought the story was about a house, not a horse.

Clear

Clear perception refers to the ability to:

- focus attention long enough to perceive relevant details clearly
- differentiate between essential or relevant details and extraneous or irrelevant details
- define and describe the attributes of an object or problem
- use past experience to analyze new information meaningfully
- perceive all aspects of a problem holistically, that is, to integrate all parts
- invest appropriate attention and time to detail depending on the novelty and complexity of the task

Blurred and Sweeping

Blurred and sweeping perception could be identified by the following:

- poor attention to form, shape, size, and space
- poor discrimination of letters
  - that look alike (e.g., confuses e and c)
  - that sound alike (e.g., confuses i and e)
- an inability to select relevant details (e.g., focuses on background noise [a car passing] rather than the teacher's voice or can't focus on a specific visual item in a picture)

Various Occurrences

The manner in which things are perceived occurs at the **input** phase, in which the student receives information from the outside world. He or she integrates this information with existing knowledge at the **elaboration** phase in order to solve problems. The response is communicated at the **output** phase. Blurred or undifferentiated perception will result in incomplete and inaccurate data gathering that will interfere with cognitive processing and communication.

Example

A student with blurred and sweeping perception may guess at words based on general configurations when reading (e.g., reads petal instead of pedal [inaccurate perception]; reads a story problem too rapidly and misses an essential numerical detail that is necessary to solve the problem [incomplete perception]).

STRATEGIES

Intentionality and Reciprocity

The teacher gives a strategy for focusing attention:

"Read slowly and carefully so you don't miss any details."

STRATEGIES TO CORRECT BLURRED AND SWEEPING PERCEPTION:

- ☐ facilitate letter recognition by linking the letter with a known object (e.g., link the letter S with the image of a snake)

- ☐ use color, tracing, or magnification to help students visually perceive differences between letters in words (e.g., "pat" and "put")

- ☐ reinforce the need to invest sufficient time in accurate data gathering by encouraging slow and systematic attention to the task

Self-Regulation and Control of Behavior

The teacher encourages the student's self-regulation:

"Before answering, make sure you have considered all the information."

- ☐ encourage students to describe in detail the information they have received

- ☐ allow students to stop periodically and redescribe the information in their own words

- ☐ reinforce the importance of self-monitoring (e.g., by slowing down, working accurately, and self-checking)

Competence

The teacher praises responses:

"Excellent Sally! Tell us how you know that."

- ☐ boost students' confidence to work independently in interpreting incoming information rather than relying exclusively on the teacher's input

- ☐ reward students for sharing strategies of successful data gathering

- ☐ reinforce a particular skill using more than one modality (e.g., read—repeat—write)

- ☐ use contextual clues to aid accurate perception (e.g., using the sentence or passage to help decode the meaning of a word)

Exploration of a Learning Situation

When presented with a number of cues that must be scanned, the individual's approach is so disorganized that he is unable to select those cues whose specific attributes make them relevant for a proper solution.
　　　　—*Feuerstein 1980, 77*

The student responds before the instructions are complete:

I know! I know the answer! You don't have to finish the question!

Systematic

Systematic exploration of a learning situation refers to the ability to:

■ approach a task in a goal-oriented way
■ take time to gather and assess all the information needed to define a problem
■ think through a task in an ordered and systematic way
■ control speed and precision when solving a problem

Impulsive

The student who experiences difficulties with this cognitive function could manifest impulsivity in one of three ways. He or she will:

■ rush into tasks too quickly in a haphazard and disorganized way without appropriate attention to what is required or without adopting a methodical approach
■ have poor investigational strategies and will not see the need to gather and integrate all the information necessary to think through a problem
■ lack self-control and have difficulty adjusting the speed, accuracy, and precision needed for a particular task

Various Occurrences

Poor exploration of a learning situation will affect all three phases of thinking. In the **input** phase it will manifest itself in a disorganized approach to a problem. In the **elaboration** phase it will result in an inability to think through the problem systematically. In the **output** phase it will be seen as a rushed and premature response.

Example

Impulsivity could manifest itself in the student blurting out answers before the teacher has finished giving instructions. He or she will engage in "trial-and-error" responses and not take the time to define the problem or look at all the information necessary to solve it. Although the student may consider all the information necessary to solve the problem, he or she will fail to integrate all the variables. For example, in piecing together a jigsaw puzzle, he or she may not consider color, shape, and size simultaneously.

STRATEGIES

MEDIATION OF

Intentionality and Reciprocity

The teacher slows the pace to ensure attention:

"Let's go slower and focus on one thing at a time."

STRATEGIES TO CORRECT IMPULSIVITY:

□ structure the environment (e.g., reduce the quantity of stimuli in order to prevent the students from shifting between one task and another)

□ vary the students' exposure to the stimuli (e.g., at a slower speed for a longer time)

□ allow students to use more than one modality in responding to a stimulus (e.g., oral and written responses)

□ repeat the instructions

□ give students a plan or a model (specify the steps) to apply to the task

Self-Regulation and Control of Behavior

The teacher encourages self-control:

"Wait a minute; let us think!"

□ delay the students' response (e.g., tell the students to think answers through before responding)

□ model problem solving by talking through the solution to problems

□ encourage turn-taking to inhibit hasty responses

□ allow students to explain the task in their own words

Meaning

The teacher asks for explanations to answers:

"Let's look at why that answer is inaccurate."

□ give students immediate feedback or insight by providing them with reasons for both incorrect and correct responses

□ demonstrate the importance of gathering and working through all available information before attempting a task

□ allow students to correct or reflect on their work and discover the reasons for their errors, if any

□ demonstrate the value of using a particular model or plan in a number of different contexts

Receptive Verbal Tools and Concepts

At the input phase, the absence of a verbal code . . . reduces the quantity and quality of gathered information.
—*Feuerstein et al. 1986, 3.7*

The student has difficulty labeling accurately:

I don't know what to call this shape.

Precise and Accurate

Precise and accurate receptive verbal tools refers to the ability to:

■ understand concepts and related words in order to interpret incoming information

■ use language as a tool to receive information

■ use language as a system for reasoning and communication in social interactions

■ listen to and interpret (process) the language, which requires a knowledge of vocabulary, word, and sentence structure (grammar); meaning (semantics); and social and cultural contexts (pragmatics)

Impaired

The student who has impaired receptive verbal tools and concepts may:

■ listen to and interpret spoken language inaccurately even though his or her hearing is normal

■ misinterpret instructions and questions

■ have poor comprehension skills that will hamper the interpretation of incoming language

Various Occurrences

The absence of specific verbal tools to describe an object or concept will affect efficiency of data collection at the **input** phase. At the **elaboration** phase, lack of understanding of concepts such as "opposite," "similar," "different," etc. may impair the ability to think about and solve more complex abstract tasks. At the **output** phase, inadequate verbal expression impairs communication of insights, ideas, answers, and solutions.

Example

If the student does not understand the vocabulary used in the classroom, he or she will be unable to interpret information. If the student cannot label shapes (e.g., a square vs. a triangle), classifying them will be difficult.

STRATEGIES

Competence

The teacher adapts to the students' level of language competence:

"Let's rephrase this in a simpler and shorter way."

STRATEGIES TO CORRECT IMPAIRED VERBAL SKILLS:

☐ determine the students' competence in the language of instruction and accommodate for their native language and/or English as a second language

☐ use language at a slightly higher level than that of the students in order to promote language development

☐ rephrase the language in a different way

☐ reduce the length and complexity of material (i.e., make it shorter and simpler)

☐ provide concrete tools (e.g., illustrations, charts, drama, sequence cards, films, maps, graphs, etc.) to explain, reinforce, and elaborate verbal information

Transcendence

The teacher reinforces concepts using examples from the students' environment:

"Name five things in your bedroom that are bigger than your bed."

☐ provide the students with specific and accurate labels for a concept and model usage of these labels (i.e., "to name it is to know it")

☐ relate concepts to the students' everyday experiences

☐ encourage active discussion during presentation of information or material

☐ relate new words to students' existing vocabulary and encourage them to think about the meaning of words in a variety of contexts

Meaning

The teacher encourages meaningful use of language:

"Which witch is which?"

☐ make sure that information is age and culture appropriate and presented in a meaningful context

☐ develop "active listening" skills (i.e., listening for meaning)

☐ develop language comprehension skills (e.g., categories, analogies, and ambiguities)

Understanding of Spatial Concepts

DESCRIPTION

Both spatial and temporal concepts are needed to define our perceptions. The uniqueness of a [precept] is provided by inserting the object or event into a matrix of time and space.
—Feuerstein et al. 1986, 83

The student has difficulty explaining the way and points:

> I'm not sure if it's left or right.

Well Developed

A well-developed understanding of spatial concepts refers to the ability to:

- understand how objects or people are physically positioned in space
- accurately locate oneself in relation to others or objects (i.e., to formulate a personal reference system)
- assess the relationships among objects or people
- use labels that describe positions in space (e.g., left and right)

Impaired

The student who has an impaired understanding of spatial concepts may:

- lack labels for adequately describing positions and relationships among objects (e.g., in front of, on top of, out, in)
- not have an established personal spatial reference system (i.e., left and right)
- experience difficulty in accepting the relativity of personal space (e.g., my left may be your right)
- lack the ability to plan the use of space efficiently and appropriately
- need to physically show and point rather than describe a set of directions
- have difficulty coordinating body parts in space
- have difficulty locating him- or herself mentally in space

Various Occurrences

At the **input** phase, spatial orientation helps an individual to accurately perceive and locate the relationship between objects and people. This permits the manipulation of spatial relationships at the **elaboration** phase. At the **output** phase, these relationships are communicated in a way that is universally understood.

Example

A student who has an impaired understanding of spatial concepts would prefer to point or physically lead someone to a specific location rather than *explain* how to get there.

IRI/SkyLight Training and Publishing

STRATEGIES

MEDIATION OF

STRATEGIES TO CORRECT AN IMPAIRED UNDERSTANDING OF SPATIAL CONCEPTS:

Intentionality and Reciprocity

The teacher provides an opportunity to experience space:

"Simple Simon says: 'Put your hands on your head, jump right....'"

□ actively involve students in games that encourage the use of spatial concepts and language, such as

– verbal instructions for finding a hidden snack

– reading a treasure hunt map

– charting a yacht's course

– plotting a route through the Himalayas

□ use different methods to describe routes and locations (e.g., mapping, charting, and plotting)

Transcendence

The teacher expands ideas:

"Which political parties are to the right of center and which are to the left?"

□ compare the use of a personal reference system—left and right—to a stable system—north and south

□ extend the understanding of how space and shape are related (e.g., in three-dimensional objects, geometry, perspective)

□ challenge the students to explore concepts such as infinity, negative numbers, the universe, and relativity

□ bridge from the literal/physical use of space to the figurative (e.g., from idioms such as "moving up" to understanding what politically "left" and "right" means, to analyzing different "perspectives" on various topics)

□ encourage the development of empathy and the ability to see things through another's eyes

Self-Regulation and Control of Behavior

The teacher encourages the student to rely on his or her own resources:

"Draw your own map of how to get to the grocery store."

□ boost students' confidence to work independently in interpreting incoming information rather than relying exclusively on the teacher's input

□ provide a concrete and personalized way of differentiating right from left (e.g., when asked to make a fist, an individual will generally do it with his or her dominant hand, that is, a right-handed person will clench his or her right hand)

□ give the students the responsibility of guiding and directing an adult to a local shop, their school, etc.; they can accomplish this by physically pointing, giving verbal directions, or drawing maps

Understanding of Temporal Concepts

Time is an abstract element and requires representational relational thinking . . . and is characterized by a need for ordering, summating, comparing, and sequencing, all of which must be produced initially by a volitional act on the part of the individual.
—Feuerstein 1980, 84

The student reveals her confusion:

Which day of the week is tomorrow?

Well Developed

A well-developed understanding of temporal concepts refers to the ability to:

■ understand the sequence and order of events (e.g., recalling a series of events in the correct chronological order)

■ understand how units of time are organized and summated (e.g., hours, days, weeks, months, and years)

■ make spontaneous comparisons between time concepts in order to gain meaning (e.g., "before" vs. "after")

■ understand how the past has influenced the present and how actions in the present will have consequences for the future (i.e., cause and effect)

■ make use of past experiences or future anticipation in order to control behavior and organize time effectively

Lack of or Impaired

The student who experiences a lack of or an impaired understanding of temporal concepts may:

■ not understand or plan timetables

■ not adhere to schedules (e.g., may be ready too early or too late)

■ perceive events out of context (e.g., might not be able to make cause-and-effect connections)

■ not understand outcomes of actions or events and thus manifest problematic behavior

■ not be able to delay gratification and will expect immediate rewards (or punishment) for actions

■ feel confused because he or she is disoriented in time

■ not exhibit systematic exploratory behavior (e.g., retrace steps in order to find a lost article)

Various Occurrences

The concept of time is abstract and requires an understanding of the sequence of events. Therefore, a limited understanding of time concepts at the **input** phase will result in poor planning and organization of information at the **elaboration** phase. At the **output** phase, students will manifest an inability to spontaneously structure their daily activities.

Example

A young student might not understand that "today" becomes "yesterday" and that "tomorrow" becomes "today." This can result in the frustration of feeling that "tomorrow never comes."

STRATEGIES

STRATEGIES TO CORRECT AN IMPAIRED UNDERSTANDING OF TEMPORAL CONCEPTS:

Meaning

The teacher helps the students to become conscious of time:

"You can't make up for lost time."

- ☐ promote an understanding of the concept of time and units of time, such as day/night; morning/afternoon; before/after; days/weeks; and months/years (e.g., monitor the hours of light or dark or the changes in seasons)
- ☐ allow students to practice understanding the vocabulary of time, such as first/last; early/late (e.g., study story sequences)
- ☐ help students to discover the value of ordering and sequencing information (e.g., use a history timetable)

Self-Regulation and Control of Behavior

The teacher provides an example of cause and effect:

"You missed the field trip because you were late for the bus."

- ☐ help students to manage time effectively (e.g., year planners; calendars; timetables; homework diaries; etc.)
- ☐ discuss cause-and-effect relationships in order to demonstrate the consequences of actions
- ☐ encourage students to plan activities and achieve tasks within specific time limits
- ☐ encourage students to attack problems using a controlled and systematic step-by-step method

Transcendence

The teacher elicits discussion:

"What do we mean by 'Tomorrow is another day'?"

- ☐ explore ways in which time management is valuable in establishing order and control in life
- ☐ discuss ways in which time is understood differently in various cultural or professional environments (e.g., an artist's sense of time versus that of an ambulance driver)
- ☐ describe time-monitoring devices as an introduction to understanding different measurements of time (e.g., digital clocks, sun dials, egg timers, etc.)
- ☐ identify different modes of understanding time (e.g., cyclical vs. linear time)
- ☐ develop an understanding of history by using time lines
- ☐ reflect on personal growth and changes over time by examining family trees, life lines, and photo albums

Ability to Conserve Constancies

[Conservation of constancy is] the capacity of the individual to conserve the constancy of objects across variations in some of their attributes and dimensions.
—*Feuerstein 1980, 85*

The student has failed to understand the constancy of quantity:

> There is more water in the glass than in the flat bowl.

Well Developed

A well-developed ability to conserve constancies implies that students can:

- perceive that the essential property of an event or object stays the same despite changes in peripheral dimensions or orientation
- identify an object even though variations in its attributes or appearance change (e.g., a person stays the same despite changes in clothing or expression)
- understand that variations are produced by a transformation in presentation that can be reversed, and that the identity of the object remains the same (e.g., the quality of clay stays the same, regardless of whether it is rolled into a ball or formed into a sausage [quantity stays the same and shape differs])

Impaired

The student who experiences an impaired inability to conserve constancies may:

- lack an understanding of conservation and reversibility of numbers (e.g., cannot see that $3 + 2 = 5$ is the same as $2 + 3 = 5$)
- have a tendency to focus only on the immediate appearance of an object without forming connections (episodic grasp of reality) or generalizing to the abstract (e.g., a glass viewed from the top looks like a circle while from the side it looks like a cylinder)
- have difficulties perceiving similarities and differences either at a perceptual level (e.g., a square placed on an angle might be confused with a diamond) or at a conceptual level (e.g., a Maltese and a Great Dane might not both be considered dogs)
- not be able to identify which relevant characteristic are conserved (e.g., is a *kilogram* of lead heavier than a *kilogram* of feathers?)

Various Occurrences

If conservation of constancy is impaired at the **input** phase (an inability to see similarities despite some differences), then at the **elaboration** phase the student will have difficulty forming categories (grouping according to similarities). This will result in inaccurate responses at the **output** phase.

Example

The student, when given two containers of different shapes that hold identical amounts may not understand that despite the difference in the appearance of the containers, the volume they can hold is identical.

IRI/SkyLight Training and Publishing

STRATEGIES

Meaning

The teacher facilitates conservation of quantity:

"Arrange these balls into as many different groups as possible. Does the number of balls stay the same?"

STRATEGIES TO CORRECT AN IMPAIRED ABILITY TO CONSERVE CONSTANCIES:

☐ initiate students' self-learning by allowing them to manipulate concrete materials (e.g., measuring rods, puzzles, scales, blocks, modeling clay)

☐ provide concrete experience with conservation of weight using a balance scale (e.g., ask the students if the two small bags of beans on the left-hand side of the scale weigh the same as the big bag of beans on the right-hand side of the scale)

☐ word instructions to focus students' attention on constancies and changes and similarities and differences in weight, size, and shape

Individuation

The teacher encourages creative interpretation:

"How many different ways can this problem be solved?"

☐ explore how individuals stay the same despite changes in age, physical appearance, attitudes, values, financial status, and social position

☐ discuss how an individual's values stay the same despite changes in the roles he or she occupies in society (e.g., a career woman who becomes a mother)

☐ challenge students to discover the concept that is common to answers that have been expressed in different ways

☐ invite students to demonstrate in as many ways as they can how to solve a problem, make a paper airplane, etc.

Transcendence

The teacher encourages application of conservation of quality:

"Which is more, four quarters or one dollar?"

☐ relate tasks to everyday life (e.g., the value of money stays the same despite changes in the size of the coins)

☐ practice measuring liquids and solids (e.g., eight ounces of sugar is the same as one cup)

☐ demonstrate how the conservation of constancies can be used in different situations (e.g., ask how they would determine if the distance from New York to San Francisco depends on the speed of the vehicle one is traveling in)

☐ bridge to perspective drawing in art or to seeing the same problem from different angles (e.g., the facts of an issue remain the same no matter what bias one has)

Data Gathering

The dynamics of the orientation towards precision is based on a generalized need . . . (which) is established by a variety of strategies very early in the interactional processes between the child and his human environment.
— *Feuerstein 1980, 87*

The student lacks the motivation to collect all data accurately:

I've got the answer. Why do you say I need to get more information?

Precise and Accurate

The need for precise and accurate data gathering refers to the need to:

- develop an intrinsic need to be precise and accurate in gathering information
- select only what is relevant to the accurate (appropriate or correct) processing of a problem once the need has been developed
- use precise vocabulary (clearly stated and detailed) to ensure the economic and efficient "capturing" of information

Impaired

The student who exhibits impaired data gathering may:

- lack an understanding of the importance of being precise and accurate when gathering data
- tend to produce work in which the data are neither precise (clearly stated and detailed) nor accurate (appropriate or correct)
- present work that is incomplete, far too detailed, lacks logical form, or misses the salient points
- be unable to evaluate whether data are missing or have been distorted
- depend on the teacher's specific instructions and resources and be unable to draw on his or her own stored information or previous experience
- lack the skills to research and extract information from a variety of sources even though the need has been developed

Various Occurrences

At the **input** phase, a differentiation can be made between perceptual difficulties in collecting data and the incomplete development of a need to be accurate and precise in data gathering. This can simultaneously affect cognitive processes, such as inaccuracies in comparison, at the **elaboration** phase. At the **output** phase this affects the ability to communicate concepts clearly.

Example

When a student makes an error in class, he or she may not be aware of it due to a lack of an intrinsic need to check work for precision and accuracy.

IRI/SkyLight Training and Publishing

STRATEGIES

STRATEGIES TO CORRECT IMPAIRED DATA GATHERING:

MEDIATION OF

Meaning

The teacher clarifies sources of error:

"You got a D on your last essay because the following details were not relevant."

- ☐ make explicit the benefits that are gained by being both precise and accurate when collecting information (e.g., the economic use of time and words will help others to better understand a message)

- ☐ explain the difference between an accurate (correct) interpretation of a question and a precise (clearly stated) answer (e.g., an essay might contain many precisely stated facts that miss the point or are inaccurate in the context of the essay)

Transcendence

The teacher reinforces accurate attention to detail:

"Review what each one of you needs to do in order to make this event a success."

- ☐ discuss how precision and accuracy have aided the overall expansion of human knowledge (e.g., careful scientific experimentation and observation)

- ☐ show how misunderstandings can be avoided by accurate communication and precise planning

- ☐ illustrate how careful planning can increase the enjoyment of an event because all important aspects were considered beforehand (e.g., catering to everyone's needs at a party)

- ☐ demonstrate how overlooking details can have universal repercussions that can lead to chaos and even death (e.g., missing a bolt on a nuclear reactor door)

Self-Regulation and Control of Behavior

The teacher draws attention to the consequences of errors:

"Be careful not to confuse a.m. and p.m. on the invitations as you did last time."

- ☐ demonstrate strategies that can be used to capture, monitor, and check data collection (i.e., to develop the need for a strategy to achieve precision and accuracy)

- ☐ encourage the students to take responsibility for their actions (e.g., in making a cake, let the consequences of using two tablespoons instead of two teaspoons of cinnamon be experienced)

- ☐ give feedback when errors are made due to a lack of attention to detail and misunderstanding of instructions, thereby developing a reciprocal need to be precise and accurate

Consider More than One Source of Information _____

*The use of two sources of infor-
mation is a prerequisite of
thinking because it is the basis of
all relational thought processes.*
—*Feuerstein 1980, 88*

**The student is considering only one source
of information:**

> I only need to know how fast
> I'm going, not how safe it is.

Well-Developed Capacity

A well-developed capacity to consider more than one
source of information refers to the ability to:

■ think about two or more sources of information at the
same time (e.g., to consider color, shape, and size
when completing a jigsaw puzzle)

■ gather data from various sources (e.g., to refer to the
teacher, experts, and the library as resources for a
history project)

■ perceive an issue from different points of view

■ examine more than one aspect of a situation in order
to see the relationship, connection, or links between
them

■ use two elements as sources of data for comparison
whenever a problem is confronted (e.g., to consider
nutrition and availability of ingredients when planning
a meal)

Impaired Capacity

The student who experiences an impaired capacity to
consider more than one source of information may:

■ tend to focus on and take into account only one of a
variety of dimensions or alternatives

■ consider only some of the information needed to
complete an assignment or solve a problem

■ be unable to recall all the facts needed for completing
a task

■ recall disjointed pieces of information and not be able
to put them together to form a meaningful whole

■ engage in egocentric behavior (i.e., only see something from his or her point of view and have difficulty
accommodating differing opinions)

Various Occurrences

The lack of, or impaired use of, two or more sources
of information is a deficiency at the **input** phase.
This will affect many of the cognitive processes at
the **elaboration** phase (e.g., summative, comparative, and hypothetical thinking). This in turn will
result in excessive trial-and-error behavior at the
output phase, as well as an inability to present the
problem in a multidimensional form.

Example

A student who focuses on some but not all of
the facts will not be able to arrive at the correct
answer in a story problem or a complicated math
problem (e.g., calculating velocity when direction,
displacement, and time all need to be considered
simultaneously).

IRI/SkyLight Training and Publishing

STRATEGIES

STRATEGIES TO CORRECT AN IMPAIRED CAPACITY TO CONSIDER MORE THAN ONE SOURCE OF INFORMATION:

Intentionality and Reciprocity

The teacher alerts the students to the need to consider two sources of information:

"In order to draw this graph accurately, we need to consider the x and the y values."

- ☐ give students tasks to work on in which they are forced to use a variety of resources
- ☐ prolong exposure to stimuli to make various sources of information more conspicuous (e.g., say: "What else can you tell me about what you see?")
- ☐ encourage students to be aware of and attend to various kinds of input (e.g., auditory, visual, tactile, etc.)
- ☐ give explicit instructions to look for more sources of information
- ☐ highlight all the relevant factors that need to be considered (e.g., underlining, enlarged words, bright colors, etc.)

Meaning

The teacher shows how errors can be avoided by using all the appropriate information:

"That's only part of the answer. What else must we consider to predict the outcome?"

- ☐ show how relative thinking can only come about when more than one source of information is considered (e.g., a poor man is considered rich in relation to a beggar)
- ☐ provide feedback for inadequate answers (e.g., "You left out some information. Can you think of what it is?")
- ☐ provide insight into the need for adequate consideration of all the data (e.g., "Don't jump to false conclusions.")
- ☐ explain how all problem solving is based on considering various options (e.g., considering the pros and cons of a decision)

Transcendence

The teacher bridges the skill to related situations:

"A detective solving a murder case needs to piece together all the clues. In what other situations do we need to consider many aspects?"

- ☐ show how nothing acts in isolation and that relationships can always be drawn among variables (e.g., the links in a food chain are affected by a number of environmental factors)
- ☐ provide practice in solving problems in which two elements must be compared as sources of data (e.g., multiple-choice questions that include distractors)
- ☐ encourage students to debate controversial issues from different points of view in order to develop empathy
- ☐ stimulate students to think of as many examples as possible in which considering more than one source of evidence is vital (e.g., jury duty)

IDENTIFY THE FOLLOWING INPUT DYSFUNCTIONS

1. Difficulty sequencing objects or events.

   _____

2. Responding before the question or instructions have been completed.

   _____

3. An inaccurate and incomplete perception of a situation.

   _____

4. Confusing concepts such as "on," "under," "beside," "front," "right," and "left."

   _____

5. Infrequent or inaccurate references to past or future events.

   _____

6. Inability to follow verbal directions.

   _____

7. Inability to recognize the same quantity of modeling clay when formed into different shapes.

   _____

8. Responding only to the auditory input and ignoring the visual.

   _____

MATCH THE COGNITIVE DYSFUNCTIONS

The student who . . .   **. . . is displaying . . .**

____ 1. responds prematurely to the first and most obvious stimulus and lacks the self-control to approach a task systematically

a. an impaired ability to use more than one source of information

b. impaired conservation of constancy

____ 2. has difficulty understanding instructions that have been communicated orally

c. blurred and sweeping perception

____ 3. has difficulty following a study timetable

d. impulsivity

____ 4. has difficulty arranging the tens and ones into the proper columns

e. an impaired need for precision

____ 5. does not take time to focus clearly on all the necessary and relevant details

f. impaired spatial concept

g. impaired time concept

____ 6. has difficulty considering all the alternatives of a multiple-choice question

h. impaired verbal skills

____ 7. cannot perceive that a square rotated on its axis is still a square

____ 8. uses approximations and distorts certain dimensions when answering

SUGGEST STRATEGIES TO CORRECT THE FOLLOWING DYSFUNCTIONS

The student's sweeping perception causes her to misread:

I thought the story was about a house, not a horse.

1. _____
_____
_____
_____
_____
_____
_____

The student responds before the instructions are complete:

I know! I know the answer! You don't have to finish the question!

2. _____
_____
_____
_____
_____
_____
_____

The student has difficulty labeling accurately:

I don't know what to call this shape.

3. _____
_____
_____
_____
_____
_____
_____

IRI/SkyLight Training and Publishing

THINK ABOUT YOUR THINKING

In solving the questions on the Work Pages, identify and explain the strategies you used to arrive at your answers. In other words, exercise metacognition.

_____

_____

_____

_____

_____

_____

_____

NOTES

_____

_____

_____

_____

_____

_____

_____

_____

If some or all of these comments about a student's thinking are overheard in the classroom, it is likely that the student is experiencing difficulty at the elaboration phase of the thinking process.

"You haven't defined the problem."

"Remember the strategy we learned yesterday?"

"Apply the old rule to this new example."

"You've missed an important clue."

"You didn't consider all the examples."

"Try to solve it without using a manipulative."

"Try to formulate a general rule from these examples."

"Let's see what's similar and what's different here."

"You haven't tested your hypothesis yet."

"Try to see the connection between those two items."

"You didn't plan that essay very well."

"You haven't elaborated or expanded on that idea."

"Give a logical explanation for your statement."

Elaboration

Elaboration Phase

Cognitive deficiencies can interact with each other, and with emotional and motivational factors, to make children school failures. But the precise nature of a child's deficiencies, resulting from inadequate Mediated Learning, are likely to be confused by teachers' and psychologists' preferences for gross descriptions of poor functioning. Feuerstein has attempted to map out, albeit fairly schematically, the act of thinking and the location of typical deficiencies within this act . . . (in order to) . . . diagnose the root causes of a child's intellectual problems. Even minor impairments could, however, have a very significant impact on children's thinking processes because of the knock-on effect onto other parts of the cognitive structure. A child who cannot be precise cannot compare effectively and this affects the ability to classify, to categorize, to draw analogies and to make conclusions.

—H. Sharron

The elaboration phase is the second step in the thinking process and is linked to the input phase—where data are gathered— and the output phase—where the answer is communicated.

At the elaboration phase the gathered information is processed. It is the stage at which work is done, the task undertaken, and the problems solved. For example, the incoming information from the input phase is sorted, organized, analyzed, and tested in order to arrive at an answer or product that can be expressed at the output phase.

A student with difficulties at the elaboration phase may be unable to see when a problem exists and fail to use relevant clues to solve the problem. The student will not automatically compare objects, add items, or use what he or she has learned previously to form connections and links with new information. He or she may lack the ability or need to give a logical reason for his or her view or think about things hypothetically. Such a student will not spontaneously make hypotheses or test them. He or she may be disorganized and unable to expand or elaborate on an idea. Essentially, a student who has difficulties at the elaboration phase perceives things as separate and isolated and fails to make connections between objects and events.

This chapter deals with such problems at the elaboration phase of thinking. A detailed explanation of how to identify each dysfunction is provided and suggestions are made for correcting the dysfunction using Feuerstein's criteria of mediation.

ELABORATION

Functions	Dysfunctions
Definition of the Problem	
Accurate	Inaccurate
Select Relevant Cues	
Ability	Inability
Engage in Spontaneous Comparative Behavior	
Ability to	Inability to
Mental Field	
Broad and Wide	Narrow and Limited
Spontaneous Summative Behavior	
Need for	Impaired Need for
Project Virtual Relationships	
Ability to	Inability to
Logical Evidence	
Need for	Lack of Need for
Internalize Events	
Abilty to	Inability to
Inferential-Hypothetical Thinking	
Ability to Use	Restricted Use of
Strategies for Hypothesis Testing	
Ability to Use	Impaired Ability to Use
Planning Behavior	
Need for	Lack of
Elaboration of Cognitive Categories	
Adequate	Impaired
Grasp of Reality	
Meaningful	Episodic

Definition of the Problem

To perceive that a problem exists, a person must first establish a relationship among the various sources of information in the given data and then note that there is a discrepancy or incompatibility in the newly established relationship.
   —Feuerstein et al. 1986, 3.10

The student is often unclear:

But what do I have to do?

Accurate

An accurate definition of the problem refers to the ability to:

■ sense that something is wrong and needs attention

■ identify the source or discrepancy that created the problem (i.e., clearly recognize and state the cause and nature of the problem)

■ state all the factors that influence the problem and identify those that are incompatible

Inaccurate

The student who inaccurately defines a problem may:

■ be unable to see incompatibility between sources of information (i.e., may not recognize that a problem exists)

■ have poor data-gathering skills and be unable to form relationships among things and think reflectively

■ demonstrate a lack of insight when assessing a situation

■ be insensitive to, and lack curiosity about, problems

■ have difficulty deciding on a course of action in response to a situation

Various Occurrences

Proficiency in all the functions at the **input** phase aids in the initial definition of a problem at the **elaboration** phase. This is an awareness of incongruous, incompatible, or missing elements in a situation, that is, that there is disequilibrium. To fully understand the problem one might need to continually return back to the input phase (e.g., to collect more data). A clear definition of the problem facilities an accurate response at the **output** phase.

Example

A student with an inadequacy in experiencing or defining a problem may tend to be passive when faced with a task because he or she is unsure of what needs to be done. He or she may be unable to continue working independently, may frequently ask that the task be reexplained, and might be unable to apply the concepts being taught.

STRATEGIES

MEDIATION OF

Intentionality and Reciprocity

The teacher focuses the problem for the students:

"What do you think you will be asked to do here?"

Meaning

The teacher encourages identification of incongruity:

"Can you identify what's needed in order to be able to solve the problem?"

Self-Regulation and Control of Behavior

The teacher stimulates reflective thinking and analysis:

"What is the flaw in that argument?"

STRATEGIES TO CORRECT INACCURATE DEFINITION OF A PROBLEM:

- ☐ ask the students to describe in their own words how they perceive the problem
- ☐ return to the input phase to ensure that all data have been gathered with precision and accuracy
- ☐ arouse curiosity in passive students by asking questions relating to the activity
- ☐ supply students with problems in which they have to identify the incongruity in a set of circumstances

- ☐ show how comparing, relating, and combining data can lead to a more precise definition of the problem
- ☐ explain how to search for and form relationships between bits of information so that the incongruity can be identified (e.g., comparison charts, categorization tables)
- ☐ encourage students to perceive problems in terms of what caused them and to isolate factors that will be most influential in remedying them

- ☐ establish in students the habit of questioning incongruity or missing elements
- ☐ provide practice in finding contradictions in arguments
- ☐ encourage students to be actively involved in defining problems by analyzing a situation systematically and thinking logically (e.g., breaking problems down into smaller parts)

Select Relevant Cues _____

[To select relevant cues] it is necessary first to define the specific goals [which will determine the person's] amount of focusing and the degree of relevance of each cue.
    —*Feuerstein 1980, 91*

The student is unable to extract the essential information:

But how can I tell which piece of the puzzle to use?

Ability to

The ability to select relevant cues implies that the student can:

■ choose and use the correct and appropriate information needed to solve a problem

■ define the goal and select from a number of cues only those that are specifically relevant to meet the particular goal

■ decide what aspects will be useful in a particular situation

■ view all options purposefully in order to differentiate between relevant and appropriate information as opposed to irrelevant and inappropriate information

Impaired Ability to

The student who has an impaired ability to select relevant cues may have difficulty:

■ finding the main points of a text

■ extracting the moral of a story

■ sticking to the point in an argument, discussion, or debate

■ finding points to substantiate an argument

■ solving problems that require discrimination and elimination of irrelevant alternatives (e.g., multiple-choice answers; word problems)

■ learning large sections of material for tests and exams

Various Occurrences

An inability to gather data precisely and accurately in the **input** phase will result in difficulties in defining a problem in the **elaboration** phase. If a problem is not clearly understood, it will be difficult to select important and relevant cues for its solution. This will result in errors expressed in the **output** phase.

Example

A student who cannot eliminate certain cues and assign preference to others will ramble off the point in discussions and have difficulty solving problems. For example, if the class is discussing camels, such a student would relate a story about his or her dog. Or, if required to select the missing puzzle piece from a choice of six alternatives—all equal in size but differing in color and shape—he or she will be unable to see that size is irrelevant because such a student does not discriminate between the various alternatives.

STRATEGIES

MEDIATION OF

STRATEGIES TO CORRECT AN IMPAIRED ABILITY TO SELECT RELEVANT CUES:

Meaning

The teacher encourages the use of mind maps:

"Make a mind map that will show all the important points at a glance."

- □ encourage "purposeful perception" (i.e., observing items with the specific aim of discriminating between them in order to discard irrelevant items). For example,
  - – compare items and discard all that are different
  - – categorize them into groups and subgroups
  - – organize items according to increasing size or chronological order
- □ provide practice in identifying the main points of a text by encouraging students to ask questions like why and how
- □ help students to discover the value of mind maps and flow charts in summarizing text

Goal Planning

The teacher mediates the strategy for achieving a goal:

"Identify specifically all the things you need to do to achieve your goal."

- □ encourage students to set clear goals when beginning a project, which will help focus attention on more specific information
- □ challenge students to describe their goals in their own words, which will help clarify thinking
- □ help students to identify the steps involved in achieving goals in order to establish a framework from which to select relevant cues

Self-Regulation and Control of Behavior

The teacher encourages a methodical approach:

"What clues will help you to solve the problem?"

- □ ensure that students understand the requirements of the task before beginning the activity (e.g., defining the essay topic before starting to write)
- □ help to instill the habit of cross checking (e.g., checking that all the appropriate information has been accumulated before proceeding with a math exercise)
- □ reinforce the need to control impulsivity and not rush through a task (e.g., in a reading or comprehension exercise, students must grasp the main idea of each paragraph before reading on)

IRI/SkyLight Training and Publishing

119

Engage in Spontaneous Comparative Behavior_____

DESCRIPTION

Spontaneous comparative behavior is . . . one of the most fundamental building blocks of higher cognitive processes and . . . enables . . . an individual to transcend his immediate perceptual experience and establish relationships.
—*Feuerstein 1980, 39*

The child's inability to spontaneously compare interferes with decision making:

> I can't decide which one to choose. This one is nice, but this one is nice, too.

Ability to

An ability to engage in spontaneous comparative behavior implies that the student can:

- move from simply recognizing objects and events to establishing relationships among them
- make automatic comparisons when approaching tasks and problems
- spontaneously search for similarities and differences among items
- organize and integrate discrete units of information into meaningful systems that are interrelated
- use and modify the criteria of comparison dynamically to suit the problem

Inability to

The student who is unable to engage in spontaneous comparative behavior may:

- have an "episodic grasp of reality" in which items are viewed separately and as having no relationship to one another
- have difficulty comparing two items (e.g., will describe one or the other item individually without mentioning the connection between the two)
- have difficulty using adjectives such as "similar," "like," and "unlike" in spontaneous speech
- have difficulty making decisions that involve the underlying skill of comparing (i.e., using relevant criteria to identify similarities and differences among items)
- make sweeping generalizations about people or events without taking notice of individual differences

Various Occurrences

The ability to compare spontaneously is affected by accurate and thorough processes at the **input** phase. It is an important function of the **elaboration** phase because it is a prerequisite to forming relationships and linking items. As such it is central to thinking and influences the way a response is communicated in the **output** phase.

Example

A student who lacks spontaneous comparative behavior will have difficulty with decision making because he or she will not be able to weigh the pros and cons of a situation (e.g., in a career choice).

120

STRATEGIES

STRATEGIES TO CORRECT AN INABILITY TO ENGAGE IN SPON-
TANEOUS COMPARATIVE BEHAVIOR:

Meaning

The teacher mediates a strategy for comparing:

"Let's determine the similarities and the differences between these two objects."

☐ explain how comparisons are made by referring to both similarities and differences according to relevant and appropriate criteria

☐ show how relevant criteria of comparison will vary depending on
the purpose of the comparison

☐ encourage students to "mentally overlap" two items to establish
similarities and differences between them

☐ provide students with criteria or attributes according to which
items may be compared (e.g., color [black/white]; size [large/
small])

☐ show how a continuum can be used to illustrate degrees of
comparison and opposites

Transcendence

The teacher encourages continual application of comparison:

"In order to choose a future career you need to weigh all the pros and cons."

☐ provide examples that students can use to practice the skill of
comparison—both at home and in the classroom (e.g., compare
characters in a novel; ads for a product; careers according to the
criteria of job description, hours, pay, etc.; or different strategies
for solving a problem)

☐ show how the prosecution and the defense can win arguments
using critical comparison of facts

Novelty and Challenge

The teacher challenges the students to search for unusual comparisons:

"Compare how an octopus and a giraffe would do push-ups differently."

☐ encourage students to make original and creative comparisons
by

– creating metaphors in original poetry

– comparing two very different subjects such as a sock and a
mother

– making unusual comparisons involving the senses (e.g., What
do you think the color red tastes like?; What does yellow feel
like?; etc.)

Mental Field

This deficiency is evident in the limitation of the number of units of information that are manipulated or processed simultaneously [or] . . . the short blanket effect, i.e., uncovering one's shoulders when covering one's feet and vice versa.

—Feuerstein et al. 1986, 3.11

The student's narrow and limited mental field affects his ability to recall:

> I studied the material over and over but I can't remember it during tests.

Broad and Wide

A broad and wide mental field refers to the ability to:

- retain a number of units of information in order to mentally manipulate them
- focus on, retain, and use two or more sources of information simultaneously
- recall bits of information that have been previously stored
- recall relevant information from past experiences
- coordinate information from a wide variety of sources

Narrow and Limited

The student who has a narrow and limited mental field may:

- be reluctant to engage in the act of trying to commit facts to memory (i.e., not take responsibility for actively integrating and storing information)
- have poor short-term memory recall (i.e., experience difficulty in remembering bits of information recently stored)
- have poor long-term memory (i.e., experience difficulty retrieving information that has been stored in the memory over a period of time)
- recall facts episodically (i.e., remember facts on one day but not on another)
- have difficulty coordinating facts from more than one source of information (i.e., be unable to associate or link information in order to make it meaningful)

Various Occurrences

Narrowness of the mental field usually manifests itself as a memory problem, which will affect all three phases of cognition. In the **input** phase, there is a lack of the need to use two or more sources of information simultaneously; at the **elaboration** phase it results in an inability to remember or extract information from multiple sources; and at the **output** phase it manifests itself as poor recall.

Example

A student who has a narrow and limited mental field may be unable to remember facts when trying to study for exams. He or she can remember parts of an event but not all of it. The student may also have difficulty remembering the details of a place he or she has visited, or a story he or she has read.

IRI/SkyLight Training and Publishing

STRATEGIES

Intentionality and Reciprocity

The teacher encourages short-term recall:

"Tell me about what we've just discussed."

STRATEGIES TO CORRECT A NARROW AND LIMITED MENTAL FIELD:

☐ use magnification (make stimulus larger) and color (brighter) to aid poor visual memory

☐ use amplification (make stimulus louder and clearer) to aid auditory memory

☐ ask students to recall or reexplain to you what you've just said—start with short passages and build up to longer ones

Meaning

The teacher mediates a strategy to aid memorization:

"Let's group this information into categories to help you remember."

☐ organize information appropriately to make sure it is understood before committing it to memory

☐ break information down ("chunking") into manageable chunks (e.g., 463921 becomes 46 - 39 - 21 [this can be done with letters, words, and information])

☐ make picture cards of a sequence of events that the student must assemble (e.g., getting ready for bed)

☐ use categorization and grouping as techniques to aid memorization

☐ use revisualization and association techniques that help make information more interesting and therefore easier to remember

☐ show students the value of processing information through different modalities in order to aid recall (e.g., by drawing pictures or diagrams, acting, singing, and using mind maps)

Self-Regulation and Control of Behavior

The teacher encourages self-monitoring of behavior by instilling good habits:

"Read, write, and repeat in order to help you remember information."

☐ move students from passive acceptance learning to actively constructing, understanding, and integrating information in order to commit it to memory

☐ encourage students to retell a story in order to facilitate meaningful memorization

☐ encourage the use of constant repetition to improve recall of information stored over time

☐ encourage students to monitor improvements in their memory by checking (e.g., How many objects in the box can you remember today?)

Spontaneous Summative Behavior

This deficiency reflects the lack of an orientation to sum up reality as a part of one's interaction with stimuli. Summative behavior makes use of both absolute and relative quantification in grouping, comparing, subtracting and even multiplying events.
　　—Feuerstein et al. 1986, 3.12

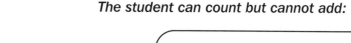

The student can count but cannot add:

> Look, I can count! I can figure out 4+5 by putting these two piles together and counting starting at 1.

Need for

The need for spontaneous summative behavior refers to the ability to:

- concern oneself with the "how many" of things around us
- add numbers, objects, and events with a clear goal in mind
- organize one's interaction with stimuli with the aim of grouping, summating, and drawing conclusions from the data
- quantify events, ideas, and materials in order to compare, evaluate, and put them into perspective
- extract the underlying concept from a summary of information

Impaired Need for

The student who has an impaired need for spontaneous summative behavior may:

- not deem it necessary to quantify anything (e.g., respond to the question of "How many?" with "I don't know . . . lots")
- "list" data without the need to make meaningful relationships or assimilate them into an appropriate schema
- count and add in a rote fashion without a true understanding of underlying number concepts
- be unable to apply concepts because of an inability to summarize data in order to extract underlying concepts

Various Occurrences

At the **input** phase, stimuli are perceived episodically and in isolation. If this does not occur at the **elaboration** phase, there is no need to form relationships between numbers, acts, or events in order to sum up information. The lack of an imposed schema makes the information difficult to communicate in the **output** phase.

Example

In learning simple addition, the student will push counters together to arrive at a correct answer by "counting" each counter separately, rather than by relating each number to another in terms of size, order, reversibility, class, and part-whole relationships. The student is thus unable to gain an in-depth understanding of the underlying concepts implicit in addition.

STRATEGIES

MEDIATION OF

Meaning

The teacher calls for the underlying math concepts:

"Is this getting bigger or smaller? Are we adding or subtracting?"

STRATEGIES TO CORRECT AN IMPAIRED NEED FOR SPONTANEOUS SUMMATIVE BEHAVIOR:

☐ avoid mechanical computations that mask full understanding of underlying concepts (e.g., sum up the relationship between mathematical processes, such as multiplication is recurring addition)

☐ practice summarizing a subject by creating an overview of the area of study and relating different aspects of the topic

☐ promote active learning of addition and subtraction by direct exposure to stimuli and allow students to discover answers rather than providing them (e.g., use concrete manipulative materials, like units and blocks, life-size number lines, fingers, etc.)

☐ provide students with study skills to summarize and relate facts meaningfully (e.g., finding main ideas; finding details; sequencing facts; relating details of cause and effect; predicting outcomes; drawing conclusions)

Intentionality and Reciprocity

The teacher affirms a summative response:

"Yes, you can group these together in order to add them."

☐ present pieces of information to students in a way that suggests the relationship among the pieces

☐ verbally draw students' attention to the need for summative behavior by constantly requesting quantifying processes, such as counting, subtracting, and adding

☐ acknowledge responses when they demonstrate summative behavior

Transcendence

The teacher elaborates a strategy for summarizing and relating facts:

"Let's summarize the causes of the French Revolution by relating all the facts in a creative pattern or mind map."

☐ help students to summarize facts about a new content area so that they are enumerated and meaningfully related to each other, as well as related to knowledge already stored in memory

☐ provide examples that students can use to practice collecting and summarizing facts in order to investigate, draw conclusions, and make decisions (e.g., buying a car, house, appliance, etc.; planning an outing/trip; examining the pros and cons of a job)

Project Virtual Relationships

The lack of need to seek relationships is an operational expression of an episodic grasp of reality. The deduction of a relationship from among all those that are virtually possible requires the establishment of a link (or connection) among objects and/ or events.
— *Feuerstein et al. 1986, 3.15*

The student experiences difficulty applying a concept in a novel situation:

I can't figure out how much change I need. Do I have to add or subract?

Ability to

The ability to project virtual relationships implies that the student can:

■ form relationships between seemingly isolated events, which involves
 - applying previously learned rules and concepts to new situations
 - restructuring relationships to make meaningful, new connections
■ bridge thinking skills to form relationships in a variety of situations that exist "virtually" or "potentially"
■ recognize a change in the relationship when one or more stimuli are altered
■ restructure existing connections between objects or events in order to solve new problems

Inability to

The student who has an inability to project virtual relationships may:

■ be unable to apply a concept learned in one area to different subject matter (e.g., not realize that adding apples is the same as adding pears)
■ tend to stick to a fixed relationship even when the stimuli have demanded that the relationship change (e.g., apply the theorem learned for a triangle to a square, a case in which the sides and angles have changed)

Various Occurrences

At the **input** phase, an episodic grasp of reality may mean that the fundamental relationship is not seen. This impacts the **elaboration** phase, resulting in the student's inability to apply known concepts to formulate new relationships, look for parallels, or see analogies. As a result, communication of information at the **output** phase is meaningless and unrelated.

Example

In the classroom, the student will be passive. He or she will not have the need to apply previously learned skills to new information to make it meaningful. The student will experience information as isolated and separate and will be unable to bridge relationships to new situations. He or she will fail to see that doing subtraction in school is the same as getting change when buying something in a store.

STRATEGIES

MEDIATION OF

STRATEGIES TO CORRECT AN INABILITY TO PROJECT VIRTUAL RELATIONSHIPS:

Meaning

The teacher gives reasons for restructuring a relationship:

"This problem cannot be solved accurately unless you extend the relationship between x and y to include z."

□ provide insight and awareness into the limitations of passively accepting a relationship without testing it in a new situation

□ show how studying is facilitated when new information is grouped and linked to existing knowledge

□ instill a need to question any new input that seems meaningless or unrelated to a topic

□ show how problem solving can be made more expedient by using previously integrated concepts and reconfiguring them to suit the situation

Transcendence

The teacher provides opportunities for bridging to new situations:

"How would you modify the method of sorting to incorporate these new items?"

□ provide practice in applying a skill to a variety of tasks (e.g., grouping by size, number, name, function, etc.)

□ allow students to form new links based on relationships between events in everyday life situations (e.g., generalize the operation of making a phone call to various types of phones)

□ provide opportunities that encourage the students to extend or modify a relationship in order to achieve a result (e.g., "You proved that all the substances formed salt crystals; what would you do to liquefy them?")

Competence

The teacher practices spontaneous application of a concept to a new situation:

"Well done! You have shown how following a plan can be used to solve both a math problem and organize a dinner party."

□ develop increasingly difficult tasks in which new configurations have to be formed before success is achieved

□ reward students for adapting relative values or relationships to suit new tasks

□ praise students for the spontaneous use of skills such as grouping, comparing, and categorizing in novel situations

IRI/SkyLight Training and Publishing

127

Logical Evidence

A lack of need for logical evidence does not necessarily reflect on a deficiency to operate logically, because the child's responses sometimes do demonstrate logical understanding. Rather, the inconsistency frequently observed in the child's responses may be ascribed to a faulty need system in which logical evidence is not prominent and pertinent.
—Feuerstein 1980, 96

The student accepts things without question:

> One should never swim when it's raining because my mother told me so.

Need for

A need for logical evidence refers to the ability to:

- internalize the desire to challenge and question the way things are
- seek evidence to support or confirm the validity of statements, facts, and events
- seek logical consistency in order to discover or resolve a contradiction
- generate questions, seek answers, and communicate explanations
- actively seek a solution once a problem is faced (when disequilibrium is experienced)
- automatically want to isolate the inconsistency in a sequence of events (e.g., enjoy finding the "odd man out")

Lack of Need for

The student who displays a lack of need for logical evidence may:

- not be able to support judgments, responses, or assertions with adequate explanations
- display a "so what" or passive acceptance attitude when facing problems
- not instigate an active search for a solution although a problem is evident
- be able to display some logical understanding but fail to apply logic to finding solutions
- remain inconsistent in formulating opinions
- respond to situations prematurely or irrationally
- be easily persuaded to adopt others' solutions to problems without thinking them through

Various Occurrences

The student who displays a passive/acceptant attitude to information at the **input** phase will have an inadequate need for pursuing logical evidence and supporting statements and judgments at the **elaboration** phase. This may often result in poor communication at the **output** phase (e.g., the student answers "because" when asked "why").

Example

Students may often present inadequate reasons for maintaining an opinion, or reach conclusions based on scant and/or contradictory evidence.

128

STRATEGIES

STRATEGIES TO CORRECT A LACK OF NEED FOR LOGICAL EVIDENCE:

Meaning

The teacher asks for justification for an argument:

"In order to convince me that you are right you need to prove it to me."

- ☐ actively mediate the importance of being able to supply appropriate and logical reasons for opinions or events (e.g., overcoming prejudices)
- ☐ provide graphic examples of the consequences of accepting ideas or conclusions without examining them (e.g., the consequences of buying a product solely on the basis of an advertisement)
- ☐ explain the importance of evidence in the judicial system (e.g., how guilt or innocence may be determined only by pursuing facts that have a logical base)

Transcendence

The teacher develops the need for logical evidence in many different contexts:

"In what ways do doctors, lawyers, and journalists each rely on logical evidence?"

- ☐ encourage students to argue and debate issues from various perspectives, bringing evidence to bear for all possible opinions
- ☐ provide opportunities for students to experience the many ways in which logical evidence is applied (e.g., in the courts, science, debate, law making, negotiation, decision making)
- ☐ explore opportunities to reach decisions based on logical evidence that may impact the students' lives (e.g., school rules regarding litter, loitering, graffiti, etc.)
- ☐ encourage the students to find or research supportive evidence in order to explain an occurrence (e.g., why a fire started or an accident occurred)

Individuation

The teacher accepts individual responses based on their logic:

"I accept both Theresa's and Jane's answers because they both justified their responses logically."

- ☐ present controversial topics and allow the students to formulate their own opinions, giving logical reasons to support their views
- ☐ acknowledge the individual's right to different views, as long as they are logically justified
- ☐ encourage students to adopt the pursuit of logical evidence in solving personal problems rather than relying solely on an emotional response

Internalize Events

This dysfunction is apparent in the pervasiveness of task-bound, concrete behavior.
—Feuerstein et al. 1986, 3.15

The student cannot manipulate information mentally:

> How can I work out the answer if I can't use my counters?

Ability to

An ability to internalize events implies that the student can:

- assimilate and accommodate information in order to make generalizations
- think in the abstract (without concrete aids) (i.e., use representations such as signs, symbols, and concepts to process data)
- mentally manipulate information and concepts that have been stored (internalized)
- use stored information to think about and solve problems

Inability to

The student who experiences an inability to internalize events may:

- rely heavily on concrete aids and sensorial input (e.g., use blocks and fingers for counting)
- be unable to hold on to or use various sources of information
- be unable to solve problems in "his or her head"
- show poor spontaneous concept formation (i.e., have difficulty formulating a conclusion)
- be unable to link present events with past and future events (i.e., be located in the here and now)
- have difficulty completing tasks that rely on previously internalized processes (e.g., knowing tables for multi-digit multiplication)

Various Occurrences

At the **input** phase the student relies strongly on concrete cues, which results in limited representational thinking. Cognitive components like planning, processing, and projecting are restricted at the **elaboration** phase. This results in an inability to communicate ideas or solutions in an abstract way at the **output** phase.

Example

The student will need to physically manipulate stimuli when solving problems and will be unable to think hypothetically—he or she will have to literally "place his or her hand in the fire to know that fire burns"; he or she cannot think of heat in an abstract way or draw on past experiences of fire.

130

STRATEGIES

MEDIATION OF

STRATEGIES TO CORRECT AN INABILITY TO INTERNALIZE EVENTS:

Competence

The teacher encourages the move from the concrete to the abstract:

"Add two to three without using blocks this time."

- [ ] initially provide the use of concrete aids and, as the students' performance improves, gradually reduce dependency on aids, thus preventing anxiety (e.g., "First use your counters and then try the next example without them.")

- [ ] encourage visualization by allowing students to close their eyes and "see, feel, and move" objects in their head as a method of understanding and integrating information

Self-Regulation and Control of Behavior

The teacher encourages the students to learn from past errors:

"Think now—don't make the same mistakes as last time."

- [ ] hide ready-made answers and encourage anticipation of an answer through questioning and probing (e.g., "What do you think is going to happen next?")

- [ ] provide oral instructions, step by step, and encourage the students to think through the process

- [ ] encourage the students to verbalize the steps or rules required to complete a task before attempting it

- [ ] encourage reflective thinking by monitoring events after they have happened

Transcendence

The teacher encourages interiorized planning:

"What do we need to do in order to make these puppets?"

- [ ] provide the students with the relevant vocabulary to generalize, categorize, and classify information in order to develop an understanding of concepts

- [ ] emphasize relationships between pieces of information in order to help the students to draw from past experiences when solving a problem

- [ ] provide practice in solving everyday problems (e.g., receiving change; paying bills; organizing an outing)

Inferential-Hypothetical Thinking

The proposition "if . . . then" is the expression of hypothetical thinking . . . and (requires) a readiness to seek alternatives by which to explain phenomena.
—Feuerstein et al. 1986, 3.13

The student has difficulty generating alternatives:

I've missed the bus and now I don't know what to do.

Ability to Use

Inferential-hypothetical thinking refers to the ability to:

- make valid generalizations and inferences based on a number of experiences
- generate a number of possible theories based on evidence, which will be tested at a later stage
- draw a conclusion from a number of similar examples (e.g., "If fire burns wood, then my hand will probably burn when I put it into the fire.")

Restricted Use of

The student who experiences a restricted use of inferential-hypothetical thinking may:

- be unable to link events or see similarities among things in order to make generalizations and inferences
- view the world as disconnected and have difficulty drawing conclusions
- not "see" other alternatives or explore other possibilities to explain phenomena
- not look for evidence to create a hypothesis

Various Occurrences

Clear and accurate perception, precise and accurate data gathering, and the ability to consider many sources of information at the **input** phase are essential for inferential-hypothetical thinking. At the **elaboration** phase, theories and generalizations are formed based on similarities in the evidence. At the **output** phase the hypothesis is precisely and accurately explained using adequate expressive verbal tools.

Example

A student who manifests a restricted use of inferential-hypothetical thinking might not be able to find alternative ways to get home after missing his or her bus. The student is unable to see the link between catching the bus and other means of getting home; he or she cannot reflect back to similar past experiences in order to generate possible solutions. He or she does not engage in "if . . . then" thinking, that is, "*If* I missed the bus, *then* I could take a taxi, walk, phone home, . . ."

STRATEGIES

STRATEGIES TO CORRECT RESTRICTED USE OF INFERENTIAL-HYPOTHETICAL THINKING:

Meaning

The teacher shows the value of generating a hypothesis:

"If Madame Curie hadn't hypothesized about radiation, X-rays would never have been discovered."

☐ demonstrate how new conclusions can be drawn by considering existing information

☐ explain how developing hypotheses forms the basis for creating links and insights crucial for the exploration of new ideas

☐ explain how making connections between objects or events helps generate viable propositions or theories in problem solving

Competence

The teacher provides practice using the "If . . . then" formula:

"If 10, 20, 30, and 40 are all divisible by 2, then 80 should also be divisible by 2."

☐ provide students with experience in generating hypotheses based on a number of proven situations (e.g., *"If* these three-sided shapes are triangles, *then* those three-sided shapes must also be triangles.")

☐ in order to make what appears to be complex more accessible, show students how to make inferences from commonalties in things they see (e.g., that multiplication is repeated addition)

☐ provide practice using the formula *"if . . . then"* (e.g., *"If* cork, wood, and styrofoam all float, *then* they are all less dense than water.")

Individuation

The teacher promotes critical thinking in justifying hypotheses:

"What other examples can you give to support your hypothesis?"

☐ explore brainstorming as a means of generating original and diverse hypotheses (i.e., ideas that will be tested or validated at a later date)

☐ encourage students to justify their own hypotheses by supporting them with numerous examples and logical evidence

☐ ask students to make explicit the thinking process that enabled them to formulate their conclusions

Strategies for Hypothesis Testing

In hypothesis testing, competing possibilities must be kept in mind, tested and either accepted or rejected before a valid hypothesis is finally selected from among them.

—*Feuerstein et al. 1986, 3.13*

The student continues an untested approach:

I don't know why, but I'm sure if I keep going it will work.

Ability to Use

The ability to use strategies for hypothesis testing implies that the student can:

- devise a suitable method for assessing a particular hypothesis (e.g., research; experimentation; practical experience)

- analyze and evaluate the validity of the process used in formulating a hypothesis (e.g., check that extraneous information was not included)

- compare and contrast all possible theories and identify which hypothesis is most appropriate in a given situation

- systematically examine a number of alternative hypotheses and, by a process of elimination, select the most viable options

Impaired Ability to Use

The student who experiences an impaired ability to use strategies for hypothesis testing may:

- be unable to devise or select the most appropriate method of testing a particular hypotheses (e.g., rely on guesses or estimates rather than on empirical evidence)

- use unsystematic or inefficient approaches to testing alternative hypotheses (e.g., walk the distance to validate the predicted shortest route instead of using a map)

- be unable to make suitable choices because the alternative hypotheses have not been successfully tested (e.g., experience difficulty in answering multiple-choice questions and be impulsive in selecting the most valid response)

Various Occurrences

Most **input** functions, like precise and accurate data gathering and a well-developed capacity to consider many sources of information, will affect the ability to develop strategies for hypothesis testing. During the **elaboration** phase, processes are used to generate hypotheses and to evaluate their projected outcomes. Valid hypotheses can then be used and communicated precisely and accurately at the **output** phase.

Example

The student with impaired strategies for hypothesis testing may fixate on a specific method of solving a problem instead of trying other alternatives. He or she might, for instance, hypothesize that a puzzle would be best constructed if started at the border. Because the student is unable to test the validity of this hypothesis, he or she perseveres with the approach irrespective of the fact that there may be more efficient alternatives.

STRATEGIES

MEDIATION OF

STRATEGIES TO CORRECT AN IMPAIRED ABILITY TO
USE STRATEGIES FOR HYPOTHESIS TESTING:

Self-Regulation and Control of Behavior

The teacher encourages the verbalization of strategies:

"Explain how you could validate your hypothesis."

☐ provide opportunities to establish the habit of checking or testing alternatives (e.g., in a science experiment, test whether or not various substances will dissolve as predicted)

☐ challenge the students to develop their own strategies for efficient hypothesis testing in order to prioritize alternative solutions

☐ encourage students to verbalize their strategy for hypothesis testing as an aid to working systematically

Meaning

The teacher reinforces the need to use a strategy to evaluate alternatives:

"How can you tell which of your ideas will build the strongest bridge?"

☐ demonstrate the value of using a strategy for hypothesis testing (e.g., using the same set of questions to test a number of hypotheses can help decision making)

☐ show how a problem can be solved effectively by choosing the most suitable method of hypothesis testing (e.g., refer to documented evidence instead of undertaking time-consuming experiments)

Self-Change

The teacher refers to the process of hypothesis testing in self-growth:

"What were you thinking about before you decided to choose that career option?"

☐ develop strategies to evaluate a set of hypotheses resulting in self-change (e.g., list the pros and cons of a hypotheses involving achieving independence, such as getting a job, borrowing money, living with a friend)

☐ help students monitor self-change by recalling previously used hypothesis testing strategies (e.g., "I thought very carefully about X, Y, and Z and decided to choose Z because . . . .")

☐ discuss how reliably testing hypotheses, rather than guessing, can result in self-change (e.g., using empirical testing to overcome self-doubt, such as vocational tests rather than subjective opinions in assessing one's aptitude for a career)

Planning Behavior

Planning behavior involves setting goals . . . and differentiating between the goals and the means by which they can be attained. The steps by which to reach an objective must be detailed, ordered in time, and evaluated in terms of their feasibility, economy and efficiency.

—*Feuerstein 1980, 99*

The student who lives only for the present is unable to plan long-term goals:

I didn't budget my allowance and now I'm broke.

Need for

The need for planning behavior refers to the ability to:

- see the value of setting long-term and short-term goals
- project into the future in order to plan ahead
- formulate goals and state how they can be attained
- construct and follow a plan in order to achieve goals or solve problems
- identify the specific steps involved in following a plan
- understand the importance of working systematically and logically when executing a plan
- modify courses of action in terms of their economy and efficiency

Lack of

The student who experiences a lack of planning behavior may:

- be unable to delay gratification in order to plan and invest in the long term
- rush into a situation impulsively without prior planning
- not see the need to plan but rather live in the "here and now," solving only immediate problems
- be unaware of the techniques and processes involved in setting, seeking, and reaching goals
- be unable to explicitly state the steps involved in solving a problem
- struggle to follow a plan

Various Occurrences

Impulsivity and an episodic grasp of reality at the **input** phase cause difficulties in setting goals, as well as planning the steps to attaining the goals at the **elaboration** phase. This will result in trial-and-error behavior, which will in turn impair **output** responses.

Example

Children who live under very poor or dangerous environmental conditions and experience a hand-to-mouth existence do not develop the need to plan for the future or predict and invest in the long term. Their environment forces them to live in the "here and now," in which planning ahead is unnecessary. Similarly, an impulsive or overindulged child whose needs are immediately satisfied does not develop the attitude or skills required for planning ahead and delaying immediate gratification.

STRATEGIES

Goal Planning

The teacher mediates a strategy for goal planning:

"We need a plan for this difficult problem. Let's define our objective."

STRATEGIES TO CORRECT A LACK OF PLANNING BEHAVIOR:

☐ model goal-directed behavior (e.g., set clear goals for each lesson and state the steps involved in achieving the goal)

☐ give students a strategy for devising a plan, such as

1. Define your objectives

2. Gather the information

3. Consider the rules

4. Plan the strategy and starting point

5. Check that the objectives have been met

Self-Regulation and Control of Behavior

The teacher provides reasons for delaying gratification and planning ahead:

"If you don't eat all of your lunch now you will be hungry in the afternoon."

☐ encourage perseverance and patience in pursuing goals

☐ develop in students an intrinsic locus of control and an autonomous attitude to their destiny (taking responsibility for your own life)

☐ show how breaking long-term projects down into smaller parts and systematic stages makes a task more manageable

☐ help students to set priorities when planning ahead

☐ encourage impulsive students to delay gratification by showing the value of investing in the long term

☐ show students how to monitor and evaluate whether their goals have been achieved and how to modify their approach accordingly

Individuation

The teacher encourages students to set and plan their own goals:

"You need to clarify your long-term career goals in order to choose the courses to take before high school graduation."

☐ foster the need to set realistic goals

☐ encourage students to identify their needs and modify and adjust goals accordingly

☐ encourage students to evaluate and review their plan in terms of time and ability

☐ explore with students ways in which their different dreams and hopes for the future may be realized through effective planning behavior

Elaboration of Cognitive Categories

A lack of verbal skills may severely affect a child's ability to elaborate certain cognitive operations. The absence of a specific verbal code to designate certain attributes of an object will . . . keep the child bound to specific tasks that he can handle on a concrete level and may impair his ability to generalize the same operation to tasks differing in content and complexity.
            —*Feuerstein 1980, 82*

The student is unable to apply a rule to a more difficult example:

I can't do division with double numbers.

Adequate

An adequate elaboration of cognitive categories refers to the ability to:

- move from a concrete example to an abstract understanding using language as a tool
- link a verbal label to its underlying concept (e.g., explore the meaning of a word like "conscience")
- discover, label, and verbalize underlying principles
- "think out loud" when working through an activity
- elaborate verbally on how gathered data can be organized into relevant categories

Impaired

The student who experiences an impaired elaboration of cognitive categories may:

- lack the correct label for a particular object, sequence, relationship, or concept
- have difficulty moving from a concrete task to the underlying abstract principle
- be unable to express him- or herself and "think through" his or her approach to tasks
- have difficulty explaining concepts in great depth due to limited expressive or receptive vocabulary
- be unable to generalize a cognitive skill to similar tasks (e.g., may be able to compare two blocks but cannot use the same criteria to compare other objects)

Various Occurrences

This cognitive function relates to the link between language and thought. It refers to the vital role that language plays in defining a mental operation in abstract thinking. A lack of verbal tools (vocabulary) and an inability to use several sources of information simultaneously at the **input** phase will limit abstract thinking at the **elaboration** phase. This results in an impaired ability to verbalize and generalize a mental operation and apply it in similar situations at the **output** phase.

Example

In the classroom, the student will only feel comfortable with activities he or she can physically manipulate and will have difficulties describing what he or she is doing. The student will be unable to apply a rule learned on an easy example to a more difficult example and will have difficulty grouping related items into categories.

MEDIATION OF

STRATEGIES TO CORRECT AN IMPAIRED ELABORATION OF COGNITIVE CATEGORIES:

Intentionality and Reciprocity

The teacher provides correct labels to describe a mental process:

"When we compare, we look for what is the same and what is different."

☐ ask students to explain abstract concepts such as love, hate, or prejudice in terms of how they view or think about them

☐ provide the students with the vocabulary necessary to describe cognitive operations, such as

   – labeling objects—square, triangle

   – describing relationships—similar, different

☐ model "thinking out loud" and describe strategies for solving problems

Meaning

The teacher provides reasons for applying thinking skills:

"To understand how the body functions we need to break it down into various parts. This is called analysis."

☐ explain the reasons for using mental processes to facilitate the move from concrete to abstract thinking (e.g., the purpose of analysis)

☐ provide practice in understanding the mental processes involved in analyzing, synthesizing, comparing, categorizing, making inductions and deductions, etc.

☐ challenge students to discover the value of being able to solve a problem abstractly without physically doing it (e.g., it saves time and energy; it is not dependent on physical props; it is essential for hypothetical thinking)

Transcendence

The teacher encourages the application of a strategy:

"You did a good job grouping those shapes. Now let's see if you can use the same rules to group these animals."

☐ provide practice for applying a concept using varied and difficult examples (e.g., find superordinate and subordinate categories when classifying information)

☐ show how a principle or operation can be used in related situations

☐ ask students to generate examples of how they would use a specific strategy to solve problems in their home, classroom, and everyday life

Grasp of Reality

Grasping the world episodically means that each object or event is experienced in isolation without any attempt to relate or link it to previous anticipated experiences in space or time.
—*Feuerstein 1980, 102*

The student has difficulty perceiving the significance of events in history:

I've studied the Great Depression but I don't know why it's important.

Meaningful

Meaningful grasp of reality refers to the ability to:

- link information into a meaningful and comprehensible whole by actively finding relationships between items and events (e.g., by organizing, ordering, summating, comparing, etc.)
- anticipate and predict consequences, establish cause-and-effect relationships, and see the implications of an action
- internalize a need to adopt an active approach to information (e.g., make meaningful connections), as passivity may be considered a central cause of an episodic grasp of reality
- control the impulsive urge to react, thus giving oneself time to come to a reasonable understanding of the problem

Episodic

The student who experiences an episodic grasp of reality may:

- see the world as a series of disconnected, separate events that bear little relation to each other
- need to revert to concrete experiences
- have difficulty linking cause and effect or seeing consequences of actions
- have difficulty placing an event into a category because each event is experienced as different and similarities to other events are not perceived
- experience difficulty with concept formation, abstract reasoning, and integration of new material

Various Occurrences

An episodic grasp of reality may be seen as a common thread in many of the previously discussed deficient cognitive functions. At the **input** phase, incoming information is vague and undefined, contributing to blurred and sweeping perception. At the **elaboration** phase, difficulty in linking information meaningfully results in disconnected or "fuzzy thinking." At the **output** phase, data may be distorted and communication imprecise.

Example

In the classroom, events are seen as isolated and separate. Links are not made between the past and the present; nor is the relationship between cause and effect established. For instance, the student will have difficulty understanding the idea of history repeating itself, or of history as the result of a complex series of events.

IRI/SkyLight Training and Publishing

STRATEGIES

Meaning

The teacher establishes relationships:

"Addition and multiplication are both ways of increasing quantity."

STRATEGIES TO CORRECT AN EPISODIC GRASP OF REALITY:

☐ give reasons for finding similarities and differences as a strategy for grouping items and making connections

☐ present tasks in which students are required to find a unifying concept (e.g., "How can I put all these blocks together?")

☐ explore the idea of the interconnection of parts to the whole (e.g., how pollution affects life on the planet)

☐ illustrate the impact of treating things in isolation and not "digging deeper" (e.g., repairing a crack in the wall without looking for its cause)

Transcendence

The teacher expands the concept and importance of relationships:

"Detergent in a stream kills microorganisms, which in turn affects all the links in a food chain."

☐ explain how finding relationships among bits of information and events enables us to form categories that make our dealings with the world more economical (e.g., individuals can usually recall seven items in a progression, but if items are clustered together, they can recall a great deal more)

☐ explain how forming valid links regarding the world allows us to add and find increasingly more complex and subtle relationships, which leads to a growth in the scope and depth of our knowledge

☐ make explicit the idea that finding connections and relationships is a creative and dynamic act and central to an individual's need to order what may seem like a chaotic, disordered, and unpredictable world

Novelty and Challenge

The teacher challenges the students to look for a cause and effect:

"What do you think caused the extinction of dinosaurs?"

☐ model an openness to "new" links while guiding the students to make valid judgments, thus keeping alive their motivation to try

☐ present tasks requiring insight into cause and effect at a level that challenges the students (e.g., in the game Clue, who killed Miss Scarlet, in which room, and with what weapon?)

☐ develop the students' natural curiosity as to why things happen by asking them to provide reasons for phenomena (e.g., "Why do stars twinkle?")

IDENTIFY THE FOLLOWING OUTPUT DYSFUNCTIONS

1. Inability to perceive relationships among objects and events.

   _____

2. Difficulty explaining in words the abstract principle underlying a concrete task.

   _____

3. Inability to support a statement or justify a position.

   _____

4. Will only check back with the model example when specifically asked to do so.

   _____

5. Difficulty grasping the disequilibrium that exists in a given situation.

   _____

6. Lack of orientation to quantify or sum up stimuli as part of a need to organize information.

   _____

7. Lack of a need to restructure relationships to form new connections (that potentially exist between stimuli).

   _____

8. Inability to extract from the rule the answers to hypothetical examples.

   _____

9. Inability to combine and link units of information in order to retain them in long-term memory.

   _____

10. Inability to set goals that are located both temporally and spatially at a given distance from the "here and now."

    _____

11. Inability to represent in the mind's eye an object without having it present (i.e., being concrete bound).

    _____

12. Cannot eliminate certain cues and assign preferences to others in solving problems.

    _____

13. Cannot construct a general rule from similar examples.

    _____

MATCH THE COGNITIVE DYSFUNCTIONS

The student who . . .

____ 1. continually asks what to do after the task has been explained

____ 2. relates a story about his or her dog when the discussion is about camels

____ 3. seeks confirmation that he or she has copied correctly despite having the original still in front of him or her

____ 4. has difficulty "thinking out loud" and drawing abstract conclusions

____ 5. has difficulty finding methods of testing assumptions

____ 6. will not concern him- or herself with the "how many" of things (i.e., the totality of events)

____ 7. is unable to apply existing rules to new situations

____ 8. relies on concrete stimuli to solve problems because he or she can't do it in his or her head

____ 9. views objects and events as isolated, unrelated entities

____ 10. is satisfied with and gives "just because" answers

____ 11. cannot delay gratification or invest in long-term planning

____ 12. cannot predict outcomes using "If...then" thinking

____ 13. fails to use relevant information learned in the past to solve a problem in the present

. . . is displaying . . .

a. a lack of planning behavior

b. an impaired need for summative behavior

c. impaired elaboration of cognitive strategies

d. a lack of internalization

e. an inability to select relevant cues

f. impaired hypothesis testing

g. a narrow mental field

h. lack of spontaneous comparative behavior

i. an episodic grasp of reality

j. inaccurate definition of the problem

k. lack of a need for logical evidence

l. an inability to project virtual relationships

m. restricted use of inferential-hypothetical thinking

SUGGEST STRATEGIES TO CORRECT THE FOLLOWING DYSFUNCTIONS

The student is often unclear:

But what do I have to do?

1. _____
_____
_____
_____
_____
_____
_____

The student is unable to extract the essential information:

But how can I tell which piece of the puzzle to use?

2. _____
_____
_____
_____
_____
_____
_____

The student's inability to spontaneously compare interferes with decision making:

I can't decide which one to choose. This one is nice, but this one is nice, too.

3. _____
_____
_____
_____
_____
_____
_____

IRI/SkyLight Training and Publishing

THINK ABOUT YOUR THINKING

In solving the questions on the Work Pages, identify and explain the strategies you used to arrive at your answers. In other words, exercise metacognition.

_____

_____

_____

_____

_____

_____

_____

NOTES

_____

_____

_____

_____

_____

_____

_____

If one were to overhear some or all of these comments about a student's thinking, then it is likely that the student is experiencing difficulty at the output phase of the thinking process.

"Put yourself in her shoes."

"Try to be a bit more empathic and sensitive."

"Don't just give up; let's try again!"

"Think of a system for working out the answer."

"Tearing up your exercise book won't solve the problem."

"Don't just randomly guess!"

"Can you explain that a bit more clearly"

"I don't understand your instructions."

"Your statement was wrong and inappropriate."

"Think before you shout out the answer."

"That's a very careless answer."

"You copied that incorrectly from the board again."

"Imagine it in your head before you try to draw it."

"Don't jump to conclusions."

Output

Output Phase

Youth workers, probation officers, magistrates and solicitors speak in amazement of the way in which children out on bail go and commit the same offence again. It seems a sort of imbecilic madness, but in fact the children lack the cognitive apparatus to fully control their behavior. Their inability to visualize the future means they cannot learn from past experience. The impulsive "situational" character of juvenile and much adult crime has now been recognized by criminologists on both sides of the Atlantic. In the Canadian penal system Feuerstein's program has been implemented for adult prisoners with enthusiastic revues from the prison administrators involved. It is precisely the emphasis of the program on reducing impulsiveness, and in developing higher critical abilities for prisoners in their dealings with their environment that has attracted them.

—H. Sharron

The output phase is the third step in the thinking process. At this point the information that was gathered in the input phase and worked on or processed in the elaboration phase is communicated as an answer, solution, or product.

The quality of certain output functions will vary with the accuracy and success of elaboration. Similarly, the kind of output response may affect future data gathering and problem solving. On the other hand, competence in input and elaboration may be marred by difficulty at the output phase.

For example, a student with difficulties at the output phase may see things only from his or her point of view. He or she may randomly guess at answers or become frustrated and give up. The student's poor expressive language may make it difficult to communicate a response, or he or she may be careless and inaccurate. The student could experience difficulty holding an image in his or her mind's eye or rush into an answer without carefully considering it first.

This chapter deals with problems at the output phase of thinking. A detailed discussion of how to identify each dysfunction is provided and suggestions are made for correcting the dysfunction using Feuerstein's criteria of mediation.

IRI/SkyLight Training and Publishing

OUTPUT

Functions	Dysfunctions
Communication Modalities	
Mature	Egocentric
Output Responses I	
Participatory	Blocking
Output Responses II	
Worked Through	Trial and Error
Expressive Verbal Tools	
Adequate	Impaired
Data Output	
Precise and Accurate	Impaired
Visual Transport	
Accurate	Impaired
Behavior	
Appropriate	Impulsive/Acting Out

Communication Modalities

This communication deficiency refers to the way the egocentric individual perceives his partner in a given transaction . . . . In this relationship he (i.e., the student) does not feel the need to spell out in a detailed and clear way what he thinks and why, since he considers this as known to the other as it is to him.
—Feuerstein 1979, 68

The student fails to explain his methods clearly so that others can understand:

I don't like your ideas— my way is right.

Mature

Mature communication refers to the ability to:

- communicate in an empathic and flexible way (i.e., to see things from others' points of view)
- appreciate that others do not intuitively know what is being thought, and therefore develop the skills necessary for effective interpersonal communication
- be able and willing to provide detailed, precise, and solid arguments in response to questions and tasks
- listen to and take into consideration the perspective of others

Egocentric

The student who displays egocentric communication may:

- relate to the world only from his or her own point of view (e.g., cannot accommodate opinions or approaches that differ from his or her own; shouts down others who are trying to get across a point)
- believe that others think the same way as he or she does, and therefore has difficulties elaborating, expanding, or giving reasons for responses
- be insensitive to social cues and, as a result, respond inappropriately

Various Occurrences

Egocentrism occurs when a student is self-centered and fails to take into account others' points of view. When communicating, the student may ignore or even spurn the needs of others. At the **input** phase there is a reluctance to consider more than one source of information. At the **elaboration** phase there is little need to provide evidence for one's ideas. At the **output** phase, this results in communicating ideas only from one's own perspective.

Example

A student will exhibit egocentric communication by dominating a group activity and demanding that everyone does it "his or her way," but neglect to share or explain his or her methods to the group—he or she acts alone. The student fails to understand why other members are experiencing difficulties.

STRATEGIES

Meaning

The teacher encourages a more complete response:

"Now tell me exactly what you mean when you say...."

STRATEGIES TO CORRECT EGOCENTRIC COMMUNICATION:

☐ do not accept incomplete responses; demand explanations to answers

☐ feign an inability to understand the students' responses until they are clear and unambiguous; query the responses (e.g., "Do you mean this, or that?")

☐ establish goals for communication and show what happens when partial messages are given (e.g., play "post office")

☐ expose students to new forms of communication (e.g., jargon or different dialects) and allow them to experience and discuss the problems associated with them

Self-Regulation and Control of Behavior

The teacher encourages precision using self-checking:

"Check to make sure that you have given us clear and accurate directions."

☐ insist on precision and accuracy by showing students how to think out loud when solving a problem

☐ foster the discipline of asking oneself why, how, and what

☐ encourage students to not just assume that everyone else automatically understands them but to check that their messages have been received and understood

Sharing

The teacher promotes empathic thinking:

"What you said is valid, but let's hear other points of view."

☐ encourage students to examine problems from various perspectives and contrast their different points of view

☐ give students controversial topics to debate and help them summarize the pros and cons

☐ allow students to role play situations that will allow them to "get into the other person's shoes"

☐ ask students to write or speak using slang

Output Responses I

Blocking may range from a lack of initiation of new responses to an open avoidance of stimuli . . . it is a response to cognitive failure which affects the readiness of the person to enter again into a situation that may lead to failure.

—Feuerstein et al. 1986, 3.17

The student's blocking response results in his reluctance to even try:

I can't! I won't do it!
I always get it wrong!

Participatory

Participatory output responses refers to the ability to:

■ try again, despite previous failure

■ persevere with difficult or unfamiliar tasks

■ initiate a different approach or strategy when a previous method was unsuccessful

■ show an interest in solving new problems

■ develop a sense of positive self-concept and confidence when confronting a task or activity that is more challenging

Blocking

The student who experiences blocking output responses could exhibit:

■ a lack of confidence when presented with challenges

■ poor motivation to attempt a new or difficult task

■ lack of perseverance to complete a task (e.g., gives up easily and quickly)

■ a reluctance to try again or to try a different way when unsuccessful at a task

■ emotional outbursts (e.g., tear up his or her workbook, run away, refuse to answer, cry, etc.)

Various Occurrences

Clear, systematic, and precise data gathering at the **input** phase will result in an accurate definition of the problem at the **elaboration** phase. Confidence in understanding what is required in a task will lead to an efficient problem-solving approach. Motivation to solve the task will ensure participatory **output** responses and help to overcome any blocking.

Example

A student who has already failed at a task is unwilling to try again because of fears of repeated failure. This results in a poor self-concept and lack of confidence in his or her ability to succeed. The student would rather run away than once again face failure, embarrassment, and/or frustration.

STRATEGIES

MEDIATION OF

Intentionality and Reciprocity

The teacher invites participation by simplifying a difficult problem:

"Don't give up. Let's break this problem up into parts and solve it step by step."

STRATEGIES TO CORRECT BLOCKING:

☐ remove any ambiguous or confusing examples that might cause concern

☐ present tasks that focus on the students' likes and interests, which will arouse curiosity and stimulate them to participate and become involved

☐ anticipate and intervene in areas of potential difficulty (e.g., break up a difficult task into small parts or suggest a different approach)

Competence

The teacher helps to motivate students by reducing their fear of failure:

"Examining mistakes can be valuable because it shows us where we went wrong."

☐ suggest problem-solving approaches that are within the students' level of competence (work from strength to weakness), focusing on the positive responses

☐ reward and give credit for attempting a new task and persevering with a difficult one

☐ allay anxiety by reassuring the students that they can produce a valuable response

☐ show that there are no negative consequences to producing a wrong answer (i.e., we learn from our mistakes)

Self-Regulation and Control of Behavior

The teacher tries to break the self-defeating habit of blocking:

"Instead of saying 'I can't,' let's say 'I'll try.'"

☐ replace the students' habit of avoiding a difficult task by motivating them to try

☐ model the process of problem solving by talking out loud when solving a task

☐ when working with students, provide them with encouragement and the skills to succeed

☐ show the students how to check their work regularly so they can monitor their progress

☐ encourage the students to evaluate their behavior in terms of positive achievements rather than focusing on failures

Output Responses II

Trial-and-error learning may actually reinforce a kind of probalistic, random behavior, diverting the attention of the individual and distracting him from the relationships to be discovered.
—Feuerstein 1980, 100

The student's random trial-and-error responses reflect an unstructured approach:

I'll do this first. Or maybe this? I'll just have to try that.

Worked Through

A student who gives a worked-through response is able to:

- solve and communicate problems systematically
- work logically and rationally through a problem
- impose order onto what may at first seem like a bombardment of bits of information
- establish a goal and devise a strategy to reach it

Trial and Error

The student who gives trial-and-error responses may:

- randomly and impulsively guess at answers
- not think ahead or plan a strategy
- tend to repeat errors and not learn from mistakes
- learn little from unstructured learning environments
- have difficulties with defining and keeping his or her goal in mind or may change strategies repeatedly
- communicate data in a random, unplanned manner until by chance he or she finds a solution

Various Occurrences

The possibility of a worked-through response begins at the **input** phase, at which careful exploration of the learning situation is necessary. Working through a problem at the **elaboration** phase means that the necessary cognitive functions are applied in defining it and finding its solution. At the **output** phase, impulsivity is controlled and responses are communicated in a planned and systematic manner.

Example

Trial-and-error behavior or "discovery learning" is an acceptable problem-solving strategy for efficient students. However, the student who has an episodic grasp of reality cannot benefit from random and arbitrary learning because he or she does not posses the thinking skills to interpret the data. If the student cannot draw conclusions, infer patterns, and learn from mistakes, then errors will follow more errors until a structure is mediated.

STRATEGIES

MEDIATION OF

Meaning

The teacher models systematic thinking:

"First, let me work out a plan for this job; then...."

STRATEGIES TO CORRECT TRIAL-AND-ERROR RESPONSES:

- ☐ model how a systematic approach to tasks results in success (e.g., in making a cake; conducting an experiment; doing a puzzle or a math problem; sorting; finding lost objects; etc.)

- ☐ show how "worked-through" responses are more likely to lead to success as inferior responses will have been discarded along the way (e.g., solving a math problem using logical calculation rather than guess work)

- ☐ demonstrate how using proper investigational strategies to solve a problem can be as important as the answer because the strategies can be used again in different situations

Self-Regulation and Control of Behavior

The teacher encourages self-regulation by asking students to create their own mottos:

"'Engage brain before putting mouth into gear.'"

- ☐ have students make up mottos in order to monitor their behavior and control random and impulsive responses (e.g., "Think before you ink!")

- ☐ develop a strategy by asking questions like "WHAT must I do? HOW will I do it? HOW can I check it?"

- ☐ encourage students to reflect on the inefficiency of trial-and-error responses and to self-correct

- ☐ show students how to critically evaluate arguments and modify them accordingly

Competence

The teacher rewards a systematic approach to a task:

"See how your strategy helped you. Well done!"

- ☐ praise the development of a strategy in approaching a task, even if the answer is wrong

- ☐ take time to identify specific difficulties of students and give individual help

- ☐ focus on concrete, task-oriented responses; move toward more abstract strategies once a systematic approach has been established

Expressive Verbal Tools

At the output phase the existence of verbal codes permits the use of more complex relationships and facilitates the understanding and communication of more abstract operations and relations.
— Feuerstein et al. 1986, 3.7

The student has difficulty with everyday language:

I...er...ah went to the watchama call it shop to buy that thing...you know....

Adequate

Adequate expressive verbal tools refers to the ability to:

- verbally communicate a response that can be understood
- use expressive language, such as having the words to say what you mean, finding the labels to describe processes, and selecting the correct words to give clear and precise descriptions
- select the appropriate word(s) from long-term memory to communicate answers clearly and effectively

Impaired

The student who manifests impaired expressive verbal tools may:

- have poor communication skills (e.g., use gestures rather than words)
- exhibit poor knowledge and use of vocabulary, grammar, and sentence structures (syntax)
- be inflexible, lack creativity, and experience difficulties in selecting appropriate words, phrases, clauses, and sentences
- show poor verbal fluency and inadequate recall of words, phrases, and sentences from long-term memory (this could result in repetition, prolonged pauses, using imprecise words, word-finding difficulties, circumlocution, overuse of words, etc.)
- find the solutions to problems but be unable to explain to others how he or she will achieve this

Various Occurrences

The absence of specific verbal labels at the **input** phase will result in the inability to think about and solve tasks in the **elaboration** phase. At the **output** phase inadequate verbal expression hampers communication of ideas, answers, and solutions.

Example

In the classroom, the student may be unable to ask and answer questions effectively. This could result in difficulties expressing ideas clearly and concisely, giving directions, following instructions, or summarizing information. In English class the student will struggle to express his or her point of view or use creative and descriptive language.

STRATEGIES

Competence

The teacher extends vocabulary:

"How many words can you think of to describe the animal in this picture."

STRATEGIES TO CORRECT IMPAIRED EXPRESSIVE VERBAL TOOLS:

☐ encourage spontaneous discussion of a variety of topics to build confidence

☐ determine the students' competence in the language of instruction in order to formulate a vocabulary enrichment program

☐ encourage students to generate a number of alternative words and praise them for selecting the most accurate or descriptive ones

☐ encourage students to use self-talk as a strategy for building confidence in conversation

☐ determine whether a difficulty is limited to the oral or written modality and provide opportunities for using both

Meaning

The teacher encourages accurate language use:

"The word 'infuriate' has been used incorrectly here. Rephrase your sentence so it makes sense."

☐ encourage meaningful use of language by discussing film, drama, or pictures

☐ provide exercises to practice accurate language use (e.g., sentence completion and filling in the blank)

☐ develop the use of figurative and creative language by helping students elaborate on ideas and describe stories in detail

☐ provide opportunities for structural analysis or decoding of words in order to facilitate a better understanding of language

Transcendence

The teacher promotes communication skills for use in everyday situations:

"Describe the unusual bird you saw on your walk."

☐ provide practice in expressing ideas clearly and concisely in everyday life situations, such as

– writing reports

– describing situations (e.g., an accident)

– role playing

– defending one's point of view in a debate

– writing original poetry and plays

☐ encourage students to interpret what they see and hear in the world around them using their own words and ideas

Data Output

We conceive the need for precision and accuracy to be the result of an interactive process between the individual and his environment, and to reflect an attitudinal and stylistic approach to life.
—*Feuerstein et al. 1986, 67*

The student's response is characterized by careless errors:

The distance between New York and Daytona Beach is one thousand feet.

Precise and Accurate

Precise and accurate data output refers to the ability to:

- communicate a response that is detailed and correct
- transmit data efficiently without omissions and distortions of collected information
- produce answers that show careful consideration and selective use of collected material
- internalize a need to collect and present information that is specific and appropriate
- develop a habit for presenting information in a clear and relevant way
- explain facts in absolute rather than relative terms and to quantify rather than use approximations

Impaired

The student who shows impaired data output may:

- communicate data inaccurately or incompletely, omitting or distorting collected facts and details
- present responses that are narrow, one-sided, unclear, or vague
- present material in a meaningless way because cognitive skills such as comparison and summation have been ineffective at the elaboration phase
- show trial-and-error responses, rushed and premature (impulsive) responses, and poor use of language with the result that data are produced inaccurately and imprecisely
- give attention to irrelevant and inappropriate information in response to a question

Various Occurrences

At the **input** phase, precision and accuracy are established by gathering information clearly and systematically. This ensures that problem solving at the **elaboration** phase occurs without serious errors. At the **output** phase, responses will be communicated effectively and precisely.

Example

The student has not developed the desire or need to work out a problem systematically and thoroughly. His or her work is continually marred by careless errors and inadequate detail. The student's math problems may reflect numbers that have been left out (inaccurate) or his or her English essay may be vague and confusing (imprecise).

STRATEGIES

MEDIATION OF	STRATEGIES TO CORRECT IMPAIRED DATA OUTPUT:

Meaning

The teacher points out the value of precision:

"Joe's answer was excellent because he read the instructions carefully."

- ☐ show how imprecise data gathering will distort communication and result in erroneous answers
- ☐ give feedback on gaps in knowledge produced by imprecision and show how this results in a poor understanding of the subject under discussion
- ☐ promote study skills to improve accurate communication of gathered information (e.g., looking for main ideas; summarizing key words; detailing important facts)

Transcendence

The teacher insists on accuracy when giving information:

"Sue, give us the exact details of the itinerary for our Washington, D.C., field trip."

- ☐ encourage students to focus on details when describing experiences they see, hear, or touch
- ☐ allow students to role play and present reports of daily events (e.g., a newspaper reporter, detective, TV personality, sports commentator, travel guide, etc.)
- ☐ analyze political speeches, newspaper bias, etc. in terms of precise and accurate delivery

Self-Regulation and Control of Behavior

The teacher encourages self-correction:

"This essay is confusing. Try to rewrite it so that each paragraph deals with a new idea."

- ☐ encourage students to give clear instructions to others and allow them to act out how imprecise communication can cause misunderstandings
- ☐ guide students' answers by providing explicit step-by-step instructions
- ☐ gradually reduce dependency on the mediator by encouraging the students' need for establishing their own guidelines for precision
- ☐ deliberately present information such as a report or a story imprecisely or in an absurd manner and ask the students to pinpoint errors in the presentation
- ☐ encourage students to rework essays before handing them in
- ☐ allow students to "be the teacher" and correct their own work in order to learn from their evaluations

Visual Transport

Deficiency of visual transport is defined as the incapacity of the retarded performer to complete a given figure by visually transporting a missing part from a number of alternatives.

—*Feuerstein 1980, 101*

The student has difficulty revisualizing an image from memory:

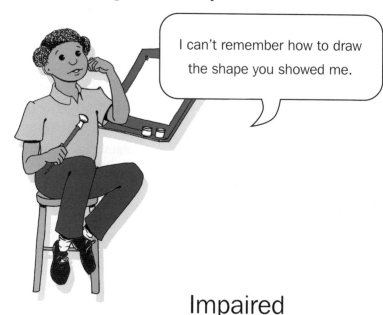

I can't remember how to draw the shape you showed me.

Accurate

Accurate visual transport refers to the ability to:

- perceive and then memorize visual details clearly
- refer to a familiar and well-established concept in order to accurately identify or reproduce it without distortions (e.g., understanding the difference between a square and a rectangle in order to reproduce the square)
- carry an image in one's mind and move it from one place to another (e.g., fitting a circle into various frames/backgrounds)
- mentally manipulate visual detail in order to internally reorient the image (e.g., imagine rotating a puzzle piece until it fits)

Impaired

Impaired visual transport could be indicated by the following:

- a poor understanding of concepts (e.g., drawing a triangle when the model is a square)
- an immature reference system (e.g., inability to describe left, right, top, bottom)
- incorrect or inaccurate reproductions of original stimuli (e.g., leaving out details when copying a picture)
- an inability to focus on relevant or sufficient detail (visual cues) (e.g., misspelling a word when copying it from the board)
- poor visual memory or recall (e.g., inability to remember how to form a letter or draw a picture from memory)

Various Occurrences

At the **input** phase, visual information should be clearly perceived. At the **elaboration** phase this information is mentally manipulated in order to reproduce it at the **output** phase. This reproduction should be transported to an area different than the one in which it was originally perceived.

Example

A student with impaired visual transport may reproduce a parallelogram as a rectangle or the number 2 may be inverted to 5. In this case, the visual information has been incorrectly reproduced. The student may also have difficulty revisualizing a stimuli without it being there (e.g., drawing a picture of a house from memory or putting together the pieces of a puzzle).

STRATEGIES

MEDIATION OF

Intentionality and Reciprocity

The teacher encourages a careful and controlled focus on stimuli:

"Take the time to look carefully and describe it in detail before you copy it."

STRATEGIES TO CORRECT IMPAIRED VISUAL TRANSPORT:

- ☐ use the verbal modality to help the visual (e.g., describe and label the figure that is being copied [visually transported])
- ☐ encourage the students to focus attention on specific details of the stimuli by highlighting certain areas (e.g., color code, enlarge, underline, etc.)
- ☐ focus on the visual stimuli for an extended period of time, which allows for clear and systematic data gathering
- ☐ show students techniques they can use to recall visual data (e.g., tracing patterns on the board with their eyes or fingers)

Self-Regulation and Control of Behavior

The teacher suggests a strategy for accurate copying:

"Let's see if we have copied it correctly by checking from left to right."

- ☐ encourage students to revisualize an image before making a physical representation (e.g., "Picture it in your head before you draw it.")
- ☐ control impulsivity by encouraging students to explain the task in their own words
- ☐ emphasize the importance of transporting visual information in the correct sequence (e.g., words are letters in a specific sequence or order)
- ☐ develop the need to check the original model to assess the accuracy of the visual transfer
- ☐ encourage the students to work in pairs, checking each other's work and explaining any errors when copying

Sharing

The teacher encourages analysis when copying to ensure accuracy:

"All the words should end in -ing."

- ☐ help students make meaning of visual stimuli by breaking them down into parts (e.g., prefix and suffix; root words; finding a square in a complex figure)
- ☐ establish a reference system to enable students to position visual images correctly in space (e.g., meaningful use of prepositions; understanding of left, right, top, bottom)
- ☐ encourage students to reread copied information to ensure that it has meaning

Behavior

Impulsivity may be manifest at the output phase. One common phenomenon is the absurd, and totally unexpected, erroneous answers offered by children.
—Feuerstein 1980, 80

The student who responds prematurely will miss essential details:

I didn't read the question properly so I left out half of the answer.

Appropriate

Appropriate output behavior refers to the ability to:

- delay a response until all information has been systematically processed (i.e., "think before you ink")
- balance the desire to complete a task rapidly with the need to invest appropriate attention to complete the task accurately (the correct answer is better than a fast answer)
- use proper investigational strategies to formulate an accurate response
- work through all incoming information (tactile or auditory) carefully and systematically in order to arrive at an appropriate answer

Impulsive/Acting Out

The student who manifests impulsive/acting-out behavior may:

- act inappropriately (e.g., clown around, shout out, have difficulty taking turns and containing responses)
- give careless answers without sufficient attention to details
- arrive at wrong answers without taking the time to gather data properly and plan answers
- give the right answer in one modality but not in another (e.g., a correct verbal but incorrect written response)
- say the first thing that comes to mind in order to impress his or her peers or teacher with a quick and snappy answer

Various Occurrences

Unplanned and hasty exploration of a learning situation will impact all three phases of thinking. At the **input** phase, it will manifest itself in an unsympathetic approach to a problem. At the **elaboration** phase, it will result in an inability to think systematically through the problem. At the **output** phase, it may result in a rushed, premature, or incorrect response.

Example

In the classroom, the student will attend to the first and most salient stimulus before he or she has had an opportunity to gather all the data available. This will result in absurd and often totally unexpected erroneous answers in various areas of functioning (e.g., in an exam or test, anxiety might cause the student to rush into a response without careful consideration).

STRATEGIES

MEDIATION OF

Self-Regulation and Control of Behavior

The teacher encourages self-control:

"Come up with your own motto to remind you to 'think before you ink.'"

STRATEGIES TO CORRECT IMPULSIVE OR ACTING-OUT BEHAVIOR:

☐ discourage quick and snappy answers

☐ after posing a question, allow students sufficient time to formulate a response

☐ encourage students to monitor their own behavior in order to delay responses and develop self-discipline

☐ develop a need to plan ahead and assess data before taking action

☐ discuss strategies for inhibiting impulsivity (e.g., restrain outbursts by counting to ten first; draw a mind map before writing an essay)

Meaning

The teacher provides a reason for control:

"Consider all aspects; otherwise your conclusions will be incomplete."

☐ ask students to think about the why and the how of acting appropriately in different situations (e.g., playground behavior is different than classroom behavior)

☐ explain that a hasty approach may have dangerous consequences (e.g., rushing across a road)

☐ encourage students to include all relevant data in their responses by listing, comparing, summarizing, etc.

☐ emphasize the importance of the means (e.g., rough drafts or the approach taken) rather than the end (e.g., answers or products)

Competence

The teacher praises reflective thinking:

"Well done! You thought that through before responding."

☐ allow the students to initially express themselves in the modality they are most comfortable and least impulsive with (e.g., spoken before written response)

☐ acknowledge the students' improvements in attempting to control inappropriate behavior

☐ reward students for waiting for their turn before responding

☐ provide the students with tools and strategies that can be used to improve their responses (e.g., listening skills; role playing)

IDENTIFY THE FOLLOWING OUTPUT DYSFUNCTIONS

1. Difficulty with expressive language.

   _____

2. Tendency to randomly guess at answers.

   _____

3. Inaccurate or incomplete response to problems.

   _____

4. Inability to memorize visual details in order to reproduce them at a later stage.

   _____

5. Uncontrolled, inappropriate responses.

   _____

6. Inability to differentiate or see things from another perspective.

   _____

7. Lack of initiation of new responses and an open avoidance of stimuli.

   _____

MATCH THE COGNITIVE DYSFUNCTIONS

The student who . . .   **. . . is displaying . . .**

____ 1. makes "silly" mistakes (e.g., adds instead of subtracts)

____ 2. cannot respond empathically or see things from another's point of view

____ 3. has difficulty planning ahead and working systematically

____ 4. draws a triangle from the model, which is a square

____ 5. has difficulty explaining his or her answers

____ 6. tears up his or her answer sheet

____ 7. rushes through his or her responses without checking

a. impulsive output behavior

b. blocking behavior

c. egocentric communication

d. imprecision in data output

e. trial-and-error responses

f. impaired visual transport

g. impaired expressive verbal tools

SUGGEST STRATEGIES TO CORRECT THE FOLLOWING DYSFUNCTIONS

The student fails to explain his or her methods clearly so that others can understand:

I don't like your ideas—my way is right.

1. _____
_____
_____
_____
_____
_____
_____

The student's blocking response results in his reluctance to even try:

I can't! I won't do it! I always get it wrong!

2. _____
_____
_____
_____
_____
_____
_____

The student's random trial-and-error responses reflect an unstructured approach:

I'll do this first. Or maybe this? I'll just have to try that.

3. _____
_____
_____
_____
_____
_____

THINK ABOUT YOUR THINKING

In solving the questions on the Work Pages, identify and explain the strategies you used to arrive at your answers. In other words, exercise metacognition.

_____

_____

_____

_____

_____

_____

_____

NOTES

_____

_____

_____

_____

_____

_____

_____

Answers to Work Pages

Input

IDENTIFY THE FOLLOWING INPUT DYSFUNCTIONS
1. Impaired understanding of temporal concepts.
2. Impulsive exploration of a learning situation.
3. Impaired data gathering.
4. Impaired understanding of spatial concepts.
5. Impaired understanding of temporal concepts.
6. Impaired receptive verbal tools.
7. Impaired ability to conserve constancy.
8. Impaired capacity to consider more than one source of information.

MATCH THE COGNITIVE DYSFUNCTIONS
1. d
2. h
3. g
4. f
5. c
6. a
7. b
8. e

Elaboration

IDENTIFY THE FOLLOWING ELABORATION DYSFUNCTIONS
1. Episodic grasp of reality.
2. Impaired elaboration of cognitive categories.
3. Lack of need for logical evidence.
4. Inability to engage in spontaneous comparative behavior.
5. Inaccurate definition of the problem.
6. Impaired need for spontaneous summative behavior.
7. Inability to project virtual relationships.
8. Impaired strategies for hypothesis testing.
9. Narrow and limited mental field.
10. Lack of planning behavior.
11. Inability to internalize events.
12. Impaired ability to select relevant cues.
13. Restricted use of inferential-hypothetical thinking.

IRI/SkyLight Training and Publishing

MATCH THE COGNITIVE DYSFUNCTIONS

1. j
2. e
3. h
4. c
5. f
6. b
7. l
8. d
9. i
10. k
11. a
12. m
13. g

Output

IDENTIFY THE FOLLOWING OUTPUT DYSFUNCTIONS

1. Impaired expressive verbal tools.
2. Trial-and-error output response.
3. Impaired data output.
4. Impaired visual transport.
5. Impulsive, acting-out behavior.
6. Egocentric communication modalities.
7. Blocking output response.

MATCH THE COGNITIVE DYSFUNCTIONS

1. d
2. c
3. e
4. f
5. g
6. b
7. a

Rating Scale: Version 1

Cognitive Functions and Dysfunctions Rating Scale _____

This rating scale consists of a list of the cognitive functions and dysfunctions. It provides the mediator with the opportunity to rate the students' thinking skills and draw up a profile of strengths and weaknesses.

This rating scale is grouped according to the three phases of thinking—**input, elaboration,** and **output**.

RATING

Mark the appropriate column with one of the following two ratings:

- **Usually** = Occurs in most instances

- **Sometimes** = Occurs in some situations but not in others

AT THE INPUT PHASE

DESCRIPTION OF COGNITIVE STRENGTH	USUALLY	SOMETIMES	USUALLY	DESCRIPTION OF COGNITIVE WEAKNESS
1. Clear perception and data gathering				1. Blurred and sweeping perception and data gathering
2. Systematic exploration of a learning situation				2. Impulsive exploration of a learning situation
3. Precise and accurate receptive verbal tools and concepts				3. Impaired receptive verbal tools and concepts
4. Well-developed understanding of spatial concepts				4. Impaired understanding of spatial concepts
5. Well-developed understanding of temporal concepts				5. Lack of or impaired understanding of temporal concepts
6. Well-developed ability to conserve constancies				6. Impaired ability to conserve constancies
7. Precise and accurate data gathering				7. Impaired capacity to gather data
8. Well-developed capacity to consider more than one source of information				8. Impaired capacity to consider more than one source of information

AT THE ELABORATION PHASE

DESCRIPTION OF COGNITIVE STRENGTH	USUALLY	SOMETIMES	USUALLY	DESCRIPTION OF COGNITIVE WEAKNESS
1. Accurate definition of the problem				1. Inaccurate definition of the problem
2. Ability to select relevant cues				2. Impaired ability to select relevant cues
3. Ability to engage in spontaneous comparative behavior				3. Inability to engage in spontaneous comparative behavior
4. Ability to internalize events				4. Inability to internalize events
5. Need for spontaneous summative behavior				5. Impaired need for spontaneous summative behavior
6. Ability to project virtual relationships				6. Inability to project virtual relationships
7. Need for logical evidence				7. Lack of need for logical evidence
8. Broad and wide mental field				8. Narrow and limited mental field
9. Ability to use inferential-hypothetical thinking				9. Restricted use of inferential-hypothetical thinking
10. Ability to use strategies for hypothesis testing				10. Impaired strategies for hypothesis testing
11. Need for planning behavior				11. Lack of planning behavior
12. Adequate elaboration of cognitive categories				12. Impaired elaboration of cognitive categories
13. Meaningful grasp of reality				13. Episodic grasp of reality

IRI/SkyLight Training and Publishing

AT THE OUTPUT PHASE

DESCRIPTION OF COGNITIVE STRENGTH	USUALLY	SOMETIMES	USUALLY	DESCRIPTION OF COGNITIVE WEAKNESS
1. Mature communication modalities				1. Egocentric communication modalities
2. Participatory output responses				2. Blocking output responses
3. Worked-through output responses				3. Trial-and-error output responses
4. Adequate expressive verbal tools				4. Impaired expressive verbal tools
5. Precise and accurate data output				5. Impaired data output
6. Accurate visual transport				6. Impaired visual transport
7. Appropriate behavior				7. Impulsive/acting-out behavior

Rating Scale: Version 2

Cognitive Functions and Dysfunctions Rating Scale

This rating scale consists of a list of the cognitive functions and dysfunctions. It permits the mediator to rate the students' thinking skills and draw up a profile of strengths and weaknesses. This rating scale translates the list of functions and dysfunctions into practical classroom activities.

RATING

Mark the appropriate column with one of the following ratings:

- **Always**   =   Noted in every instance

- **Mostly**   =   Occurs with regularity

- **Sometimes**   =   Occurs in some situations but not in others

- **Rarely**   =   Very seldom in evidence

- **Never**   =   Not in evidence at all

THINKING SKILL	ALWAYS	MOSTLY	SOMETIMES	RARELY	NEVER
1. When faced with a problem, the student gathers the necessary information in a careful manner (i.e., is thorough and attends to details).					
2. The student approaches new information in a controlled, systematic way (i.e., does not react impulsively to stimuli; takes time to think things over).					
3. The student is able to understand new verbal information adequately (i.e., understands what is said; can identify objects or events if their names or descriptions are given).					
4. The student knows left from right, top from bottom, as well as being able to relate to (locate) objects and events in his or her world (e.g., next to, around the corner, etc.).					
5. The student has a sense of time and understands and differentiates among time concepts such as now, in one hour's time, 8 o'clock, yesterday, tomorrow, next week, last year, etc.					
6. The student understands that the size, shape, or quantity of an object stays the same even if its position changes (i.e., is able to conserve constancies). Example 1. The amount of water moved from a tall to a fat glass may look like less in the fat glass, but the student knows it is still the same amount. Example 2. Once the student has understood the concept of multiplication, he or she is able to apply it to examples, regardless of how the sum is presented.					
7. When beginning a task, the student makes sure that his or her information is precise and accurate (e.g., checks that copying from board is accurate).					
8. When the student is confronted with a problem, he or she is able to consider two or more sources of information that might be used together in solving the problem (e.g., in plotting a graph, both the x and the y axes need to be considered; in working out an area, length and width must be considered).					
9. The student generally is able to identify a problem and describe it clearly (i.e., is able to see what the tasks requires him or her to do).					
10. The student is able to choose and use the correct and appropriate information needed to attempt a problem (i.e., can decide what aspects of the given information will be useful).					
11. The student makes comparisons when approaching tasks and problems (e.g., sees similarities and differences between different types or aspects of problems and approaches, compares different characters in a story, etc.).					
12. The student can solve problems mentally, without using concrete aids (i.e., is able to think abstractly; can argue about possibilities, future outcomes, alternative approaches).					
13. The student actively tries to sequence and summarize new information and events in order to organize them (e.g., when explaining an event or telling a story, it is clear that he or she has extracted or summarized the main idea).					
14. The student is able to apply rules to make new associations and insights.					

THINKING SKILL	ALWAYS	MOSTLY	SOMETIMES	RARELY	NEVER
15. The student actively looks for explanations to problems and is able to argue logically to support possible answers (i.e., uses logical evidence to support arguments or conclusions).					
16. The student is able to link new information to knowledge previously acquired in order to solve a problem (i.e., can build on experiences or past learning).					
17. The student is able to formulate a rule from a number of examples.					
18. The student can test a hypothesis using a variety of approaches.					
19. The student is able to construct and follow a plan in order to solve problems (i.e., can develop a logical plan).					
20. When solving a problem, the student is able to explain in detail what he or she is doing.					
21. The student has a good understanding of how things are connected and related in his or her world (i.e., does not see things as isolated and episodic; sees a relationship between what has been done and the present, or what is being done now, and future outcomes).					
22. The student's answers, verbal or written, are clear, precise, and easy to understand.					
23. The student shows an interest in attempting to solve new problems.					
24. The student thinks ahead and uses a strategy before attempting an answer (i.e., does not use trial-and-error responses; thinks about or plans an answer carefully).					
25. The student is able to communicate answers clearly and effectively (i.e., uses appropriate language; has good vocabulary).					
26. The student is accurate and precise when answering a question or expressing him- or herself in writing or in explaining the solution to problems.					
27. The student is able to think about a problem in his or her head without having to constantly refer back to the given example.					
28. The student's answers and actions are planned and controlled (i.e., doesn't answer or act impulsively; thinks before he or she acts).					

IRI/SkyLight Training and Publishing

Glossary

abstract   ideas or concepts that are not concrete

affective   pertaining to emotions and feelings

autonomy   self-sufficiency and independence of the individual

closure   completion

cognitive   pertaining to thinking skills or mental processes

concepts   ideas; general notions

cooperative learning   working together for mutual benefit

culture   According to Feuerstein, culture does not refer to a closed or static list of behaviors, but to a *process* by which knowledge, values, and beliefs are transmitted across generations.

decentrate   the ability to see things from different perspectives

disequilibrium   a state of imbalance; a problem

dysfunctional   impaired or disabled

empathy   understanding and identifying with another's feelings; putting oneself in another's shoes

empower   to develop an ability to act autonomously

episodic grasp of reality   the perception of reality as consisting of separate, isolated, and unrelated entities

external locus of control   attributing success or failure to outside forces; not taking responsibility for one's successes or failures

function   a specific task

hypothesis   a supposition made as a basis for reasoning

impulsivity   rushing into a task and acting without thought of the consequences

infer   to deduce or conclude from a variety of examples

interaction   the interconnection, interdependence, and movement among objects, events, ideas, or people

interiorization   solving a problem in one's head

internal locus of control   taking responsibility for one's own success or failure

intrinsic   the basic nature of a person or thing

intrinsic motivation   a desire to complete a task for its own value rather than for external rewards

lateral thinking   problem solving in which the individual attempts to view the problem from many angles rather than to search for a direct, straightforward solution

logical evidence   reasons available as proof to substantiate facts

manipulate   to skillfully arrange (objects, facts, subjects, or emotions)

mediator According to Feuerstein, a mediator is an experienced, intentioned, and active human being, prototypically the parent and later the teacher, who interacts with the child and interprets and explains both present and historic reality to him or her. The quality of this interaction will influence the degree of later learning or cognitive modifiability of which the individual will be capable.

mediatee the person who receives and interacts with the mediator

mental act a stage of thinking

metacognition thinking about thinking; an awareness and understanding of one's thought processes and behavior

mental field the area of operating in one's mind

mental image a picture in one's mind

modality the mode or manner in which something is expressed or communicated (e.g., MLE can be expressed in a number of modalities such as language, gesture, observation, etc.)

modeling demonstrating a type of behavior or action in order to illustrate something

modifiable having the potential to change

multiculturalism the diversity of cultures

needs system the internalized environmental demands that are made on an individual

operationalize to show the application or use of

peer tutoring learning from fellow students

rote recall the regurgitation of facts without necessarily understanding them

revisualize to make visible in one's mind a distinct mental image

self-disclosure expressing one's feelings and opinions

self-monitor assessing and regulating one's behavior

stimuli any objects, events, or ideas in the environment

summation finding the total; giving a résumé

virtual relationship the essence of a relationship, rather than the actuality

visual transport moving a mental image in one's mind

visual image seeing a picture in one's mind

References

Feuerstein, R. 1980. *Instrumental Enrichment*. Baltimore, Md.: University Park Press.

Feuerstein, R. 1979. *The dynamic assessment of retarded performers*. Baltimore, Md.: University Park Press.

Feuerstein R., and M. Jensen. 1980. Instrumental Enrichment: Theoretical basis, goals and instruments. *Educational Forum* 44, n. 4: 401–23.

Feuerstein, R., and others. 1986. *L.P.A.D.: Learning potential assessment device manual*. Jerusalem: Hadassah-Wizo-Canada Research Institute.

Feuerstein, R., and others. 1982. "Learning to learn: MLE and IE." *Special Services in the Schools* 3 (l–2): 49–82.

Feuerstein, R., Y. Rand, and M. Hoffman. 1979. *The dynamic assessment of retarded performers, the learning potential assessment device, theory instruments and techniques*. Baltimore, Md.: University Park Press.

Feuerstein, R., Y. Rand, M. Hoffman, and R. Miller. 1980. *Instrumental Enrichment: An intervention program for cognitive modifiability*. Baltimore, Md.: University Park Press.

Gilg, J. E. 1990. The use of mediated learning to enhance the educational effectiveness of school programs for high-risk youth. *International Journal of Cognitive Education and Mediated Learning* 1 (1): 63–71.

Greenberg, K. H. 1990. *Cognet: Parent's manual*. University of Tennessee. (unpublished)

Greenberg, K. H. 1990. Mediated learning in the classroom. *International Journal of Cognitive Education and Mediated Learning* 1 (81): 33–44.

Greenberg, K. H., and S. A. Kaniel. 1990. Thousand year transition for Ethiopian immigrants to Israel: The effects of modifiability, mediated learning and cultural transmission. *International Journal of Cognitive Education and Mediated Learning* 1 (2): 137–42.

Hopson, B., and M. Scally. 1981. *Life skills teaching*. London: McGraw-Hill.

Kozulin, A. 1990. Mediation: Psychological activity and psychological tools. *International Journal of Cognitive Education and Mediated Learning* 1 (2): 151–59.

Savell, J. M., and others. 1986. Empirical status of Feuerstein's "Instrumental Enrichment" (FIE) techniques as a method of teaching thinking skills. *Review of Educational Research* 56 (4): 383–409.

Sharron, H. 1987. *Changing children's minds: Feuerstein's revolution in the teaching of intelligence*. London: Souvenir Press.

Skuy, M., and others. 1990. Combining Instrumental Enrichment and creativity/socioemotional development for disadvantaged gifted adolescents in Soweto. Pt. 1. *International Journal of Cognitive Education and Mediated Learning* 1 (1): 25–31.

Skuy, M., and others. 1990. Combining Instrumental Enrichment and creativity/socioemotional development for disadvantaged gifted adolescents in Soweto. Pt. 2. *International Journal of Cognitive Education and Mediated Learning* 1 (2): 93–102.

Skuy, M., and M. Mentis. 1992. Applications and adaptations of Feuerstein's Instrumental Enrichment programme among the disadvantaged population in South Africa. In *Cognition and educational practice: An international perspective, Volume I (Part B),* edited by J. Carlson, 105–27. Greenwich, Conn.: JAI Press.

Skuy, M., and M. Mentis. 1990. *Application of instrumental enrichment programme in South Africa*. Proceedings of the HSRC Conference on Cognitive Development, 1 November, in Pretoria, South Africa.

Tzuriel, D., and Z. Eran. 1990a. Inferential cognitive modifiability of kibbutz young children as a function of mother-child Mediated Learning Experience (MLE) interactions. *International Journal of Cognitive Education and Mediated Learning* 1 (2): 103–17.

Tzuriel, D., and Z. Eran. 1990b. Mediated Learning Experience and cognitive modifiability: Testing the effects of distal and proximal factors by structural equation model. *International Journal of Cognitive Education and Mediated Learning* 1 (2): 119–35.

About the Cognitive Research Program Manual Team

(From left to right: Angela Arnott, Marténe Mentis, Marilyn Dunn, Mervyn Skuy, Mandia Mentis, and Fleur Durbach.)

Mervyn Skuy

Mervyn Skuy is Professor and Head of the Division of Specialized Education at the University of the Witwatersrand in South Africa. He has a Ph.D. in psychology and is a clinical and educational psychologist. As the founder and director of the Cognitive Research Program at the university, he has initiated and led numerous research, training, and community projects in Feuerstein's approaches, including the Learning Potential Assessment Device, Instrumental Enrichment, and Mediated Learning Experience. He has published and presented extensively and internationally. His current interest is in the link between thinking skills and multicultural integration.

Mandia Mentis

Mandia Mentis, an educational psychologist, works in the areas of teacher training, life-skills education, and cognitive research. She has coordinated numerous projects of the Cognitive Research Program, implementing Feuerstein's Instrumental Enrichment, Mediated Learning Experience, and Learning Potential Assessment Device in remedial, counseling, pastoral, school, parenting, and teacher-training contexts. A lecturer in the Division of Specialized Education of the University of the Witwatersrand, she holds a master's degree in Educational Psychology, a higher diploma in Education, and is working on her Ph.D.

Angela Arnott

Angela Arnott has been involved in research for eleven years, six of which in education. As a researcher in the Cognitive Research Program for two years, she was involved with projects relating to Mediated Learning Experience in colleges and schools. She is currently working as a senior policy analyst in a Policy Support Unit that advises provincial and national education departments on policy information issues. She has an honors degree in sociology.

Marilyn Dunn

Marilyn Dunn has been working in the field of education for twenty-six years, and also has various qualifications in business. For the past ten years she has been a researcher for the Cognitive Research Program, implementing Feuerstein's Instrumental Enrichment and Mediated Learning Experience with gifted disadvantaged pupils in South African black townships. She is vice-principal of King David High School and heads the Science, Technology, and Computer departments. She holds a master's degree in education and is presently working on her Ph.D.

Fleur Durbach

Fleur Durbach has been involved in remedial education for sixteen years. She is a researcher in the Cognitive Research Program, and has applied Feuerstein's Instrumental Enrichment and Mediated Learning Experience extensively in the areas of remedial and preschool education, as well as in parenting skills. She is head of the Junior Elementary Department at Blairgowrie School and tutors remedial teachers in the Division of Specialized Education, University of the Witwatersrand.

Marténe Mentis

Marténe Mentis has worked in the areas of education, business, and desktop publishing. She has worked as a researcher with the Cognitive Research Program, and has applied Feuerstein's Instrumental Enrichment and Mediated Learning Experience in secondary and tertiary educational settings. In addition, she implemented a research project using Feuerstein's program in a small mining town in South Africa. She currently teaches the Foundation Course in Visual Literacy in the Faculty of Arts, University of the Witwatersrand. She holds a degree in Fine Art and a higher diploma in Teaching, and is currently completing her master's degree in education.

Index

NOTES

NOTES

NOTES

NOTES

NOTES

NOTES

Learn from Our Books *and* from Our Authors!

Bring Our Author/Trainers to Your District

At IRI/SkyLight, we have assembled a unique team of outstanding author/trainers with international reputations for quality work. Each has designed high-impact programs that translate powerful new research into successful learning strategies for every student. We design each program to fit your school's or district's special needs.

Training Programs

IRI/SkyLight's training programs extend the renewal process by helping educators move from content-centered to mind-centered classrooms. In our highly interactive workshops, participants learn foundational, research-based information and teaching strategies in an instructional area that they can immediately transfer to the classroom setting. With IRI/SkyLight's specially prepared materials, participants learn how to teach their students to learn for a lifetime.

Network for Systemic Change

Through a partnership with Phi Delta Kappa, IRI/SkyLight offers a Network for site-based systemic change: *The Network of Mindful Schools*. The Network is designed to promote systemic school change as possible and practical when starting with a renewed vision that centers on *what* and *how* each student learns. To help accomplish this goal, Network consultants work with member schools to develop an annual tactical plan and then implement that plan at the classroom level.

Training of Trainers

The Training of Trainers programs train your best teachers, those who provide the highest quality instruction, to coach other teachers. This not only increases the number of teachers you can afford to train in each program, but also increases the amount of coaching and follow-up that each teacher can receive from a resident expert. Our Training of Trainers programs will help you make a systemic improvement in your staff development program.

To receive a FREE COPY of the IRI/SkyLight catalog or more information about trainings offered through IRI/SkyLight, contact **CLIENT SERVICES** at

TRAINING AND PUBLISHING, INC.
2626 S. Clearbrook Dr., Arlington Heights, IL 60005
800-348-4474 • 847-290-6600 • FAX 847-290-6609

There are
one-story intellects,
two-story intellects, and three-story
intellects with skylights. All fact collectors, who
have no aim beyond their facts, are one-story men. Two-story men
compare, reason, generalize, using the labors of the fact collectors as
well as their own. Three-story men idealize, imagine,
predict—their best illumination comes from
above, through the skylight.
—*Oliver Wendell*
Holmes

IRI SkyLight
TRAINING AND PUBLISHING, INC.